The Presentation Playbook

Win the war for **attention** and make an **impact**

Kris Flegg

Rethink

First published in Great Britain in 2024
by Rethink Press (www.rethinkpress.com)

Contents

Why Are You Reading This?

Maybe you *suck* at presentations. Maybe you don't. Regardless, I'm going to make some assumptions about you. Stop me if I'm wrong.

- You want your presentations to make an impact. (Hardly a huge leap, given you're here.)

- The moment you hit 'present' on your PowerPoint, you want the time and effort you've invested in it to be meaningful.

- You want to reach that final slide knowing that your presentation meant something. You want to see in your audience's shimmering eyes that they're ready to invest, change their ways or follow you to the ends of the earth.

- You want to turn that pit in your stomach as you enter the room into a sense of calm, quiet confidence that you'll do yourself justice.

- Maybe you're just terrified of embarrassing yourself with an awful presentation.

One or more of these should resonate with you, even if it's just the last one. If they don't, this book isn't for you. You *have* to care.

Whether you're a seasoned professional public speaker or giving your first presentation, a corporate trainer facilitating a group of people that really don't want to be there or a newly appointed manager speaking to the board for the first time, the challenge is the same. You want your audience to remember your presentation. You want to make a difference.

And yet, the harsh reality is… *Most presentations fail.*

Not the 'throwing rocks and booing the presenter' kind of failure, but a slow decline into indifference, your audience's faces glazing over, your words falling flat as you click through slide after slide. In a 2022 *Forbes* article, Jane Hanson says, 'Four out of five business professionals stopped paying attention during the last presentation they watched.' And no one who wasn't paying attention is going to give you their time, their consideration and their hard-earned cash. You've wasted their time and you've wasted yours.

The sad truth is that most presenters have almost no impact on their audience. Over the last ten years, I've had the unique experience of working behind the scenes with clients to develop presentations across almost every industry. From employee workshops and boardroom presentations to $500 million tenders, high-energy Tony Robbins-style speakers to CEOs trying to engage their team – people from every walk of life have stepped into my office and asked for help with their next presentation.

I've witnessed the build up, the moments of truth and the results as presenters attempt to make an impact. I've been the first person they call after leaving the venue. I've seen almost every scene play out: a quietly spoken introvert moving a room, standing ovations, stunned silences. I've watched a client walk up to the stage to deliver a TED Talk at the Sydney Opera House, her first ever presentation, and felt as nervous as if I were up there myself. (If you want to see how this went, look up Nadine Champion's closing talk at TEDx Sydney 2015.)

I kept asking myself: what happens before and during a presentation's delivery that sets these few great presenters apart from the rest? I became obsessed with finding the commonalities that create successful presentations, and my unique experience gave me access to the hundreds of different approaches these presenters took to get there. I compared all the variables between average performances and those that cut through and made an impact.

I learned that the presenters who made an impact hadn't all read the same article; they weren't using the same tips and tricks; the topics they presented were completely different to one another. Some were in sales and others were facilitating workshops. There were highly experienced presenters and newer ones. But as I reflected on their differences, I also started to see patterns.

These varied presenters, who'd never met, were almost identical in certain traits. There were extraordinary similarities in their process and even their vocabulary. They didn't rely on superficial hacks like picturing their audience naked. While most presenters were putting their audiences to sleep, these impactful few were getting them on their feet, excited and ready to take action.

When it came to delivering, they seemed at ease and found ways to engage their audience. They cultivated far better connections, and when we saw them live, they generated pertinent questions at the end of their presentations. (You've likely sat through enough dull talks to know that this rarely happens.)

Despite their differences, there is a single commonality that differentiates the successful from the rest. Something that leads them to common philosophies and practices that drive better outcomes. And that's what this book can give you. No 'hacks', just good practices that will take your next presentation to the next level. To be clear, the next level isn't a TED Talk. This won't turn you into a professional public speaker, but it will give you the tools to keep your audience engaged, stop them switching off and get them to listen to what you have to say.

Your presentations will change from being a waste of time to making an impact in your life.

I've distilled this secret down into a set of five simple principles that you can follow to enjoy transformative success. They will give you clarity on your role and your task, influencing every aspect of your presentation – its content, your language and the questions you need to ask yourself to create a presentation that actually gets people engaged and talking.

Once you have these principles, you still need to organise your ideas, create a presentation and deliver it. Considering how essential presentations are to people's careers, it's insane that there is no standard practice for creating and delivering quality presentations.

I am also going to share with you the exact presentation creation process that we at Presentation Design Co use to take initial ideas all the way through content creation, structure and design. It's the production method that we use every day – one that's efficient, tested and reliable.

This book can make you successful. It can transform your presentation outcomes from snooze fest to invest. You'll see it in your audience's eyes – a spark, an idea, a shift in perspective.

Everyone has a foundation, a starting point from which they need to find the right pieces to build a path to presenting more naturally and effectively. The following pages contain the insights, gathered from my unique position working with hundreds of presenters, to set you on that path. You will discover steps and processes to hone your focus on improving key aspects of your presentations.

My passionate goal is to support and empower you so that you can enjoy the rewards of being an impactful presenter. Although we may never meet, I'm excited that even just a few of the steps here might lead you in that direction.

The ideas in this book helped me become the best presenter I could be. I hope they do the same for you.

PART ONE
MINDSET

E very presentation is an opportunity to make an impact and change the future. It's up you to make it happen. The alternative? You bore people to death with another crappy PowerPoint.

1
The Lightbulb Moment

This is when you say, 'Enough is enough.' Whether you're reading this as a terrible presenter, a mediocre one, or just someone who could do better, this is your chance to finally do something about it.

An afternoon in presentation hell...

It's 2:35pm at a financial services conference on Australia's sunny Gold Coast. We've now moved into the 'after lunch' presentation time slot, also known as the 'Dead Zone'.

The attendees, full from the endless buffet, were enjoying some great conversations with other conference attendees just minutes ago. Then, out of nowhere, their networking is cut short and they are ordered into a dimly lit room for the next round of presentations.

It's painfully obvious that they aren't there by choice. Most of them have the bland look of being inconvenienced. They take their seats, check their phones and settle in with rather low expectations. Their only job for the next few hours is to try to stay awake. They watch as the presenter fumbles with the PowerPoint clicker while the next brightly coloured logo slide springs to life on the screen.

One sentence blends into the next, and half an hour later, we're up to slide twenty-four. Or is it thirty-four? No one really knows – as ever, everything after the first few points has started to feel like the same worn-out experience.

The presentation isn't special. It isn't interactive. It isn't fun. In fact, it could be from any of the day's speakers. Energy levels in the room are at an all-time low. Any chance of engagement was lost a long time ago, somewhere between the shaky introduction and the long-winded explanation of a graph that everyone will forget the moment it's replaced by the next.

Like the final moments of a one-sided sporting match, it's just a matter of watching the clock wind down. (Experience tells us there'll be a small spike of energy towards the end, as the audience tries to figure out if it's finished for good.) The speaker's voice loses pitch and poise as they realise this is a lost cause. Finally, the presentation is over. Silence, followed by a small awkward clap, no questions, and the slow march to the next room (where the process will inevitably repeat itself). It's another of those presentations that will fall into the melee of 'Tick the box, job done', but has ultimately failed in its purpose.

Does this sound familiar? It's painful to admit, but I was that presenter.

That was my awful experience. Despite wanting to make an impact, I had failed. I was devastated and embarrassed, but that presentation at the Gold Coast conference was my lightbulb moment. It marked the day I decided to change.

I was fed up with being boring. I promised that I would step away from presenting just like everyone else. I desperately wanted to do better and that experience became my fuel. My passion to improve and the work that I do now all stems from that chastening experience. Over the next few years, I pushed myself and worked hard to improve. I read a lot, enrolled in courses, went deep researching great presenters and took every opportunity I could to present.

With a fresh new perspective, I started to understand the key elements of presenting and started to see better results. I went from being average to slightly better than average. I attended more courses, I read more books, I dabbled in public speaking, and slowly, bit by bit, I continued to improve.

Presenting took on a new role when I left a career in banking to pitch my own start-up. There wasn't a company to hide behind, so I couldn't blame marketing for giving me a terrible deck. It was all me and the stakes were suddenly obscenely high. Those presenting skills weren't just helpful anymore – they were vital.

During this time, I could see friends and old colleagues stuck in the same situation I had been, experiencing the same average results. I felt I had some of the answers and was eager to help other people become unstuck and achieve greater success with their presentations. This was the start of my agency – Presentation Design Co – and over the last ten years, I've been at the coalface with the team helping people deliver better presentations that actually make an impact.

The silent failure

My own experience, and the opportunity of working with business presentations every day, helps give me a unique insight into the reality that with few exceptions, most business presentations fail. But here's the thing: these failures are subtle. They don't usually fail spectacularly. Instead, they simply fade away into a box of 'meh'. No matter the intentions of the speakers, many simply miss the opportunity to deliver.

We've all seen so many of these that it's become an accepted practice for sub-standard presentations to be a normal part of the business environment. But they don't fulfil their potential. They make no impact. They don't change anything.

Swap rules for process

Presenters don't choose to fail. They just don't know how to do it right. To enjoy success, they feel it can take years or even decades to become a world-class presenter. However, not everyone needs to be world-class right away, or even ever.

Just by starting to try to get better, you can start to achieve a huge difference. I will share ways to quickly and immediately transform what you are doing. You can make significant improvements straight away, starting with your next presentation. Chances are there are things you're doing – that you may not be consciously aware of – which are slowly *poisoning* your presentation.

Rather than inflicting these on your audience, let's try and call them out, then improve your presentation by eliminating them. There may be some small mindset tweaks that are obvious when we point them out but will serve as a catalyst for you to develop new ideas, generate way more interesting content or simple ways to improve a slide's effectiveness.

If you feel stuck, simply try some of the ideas I suggest to improve. That alone will put you ahead of 85% of presenters. Remember that your next presentation doesn't need to be a world-class TED Talk, just a bit better than what you're doing already. Embrace your new mindset, follow the process, and it will replace the try/fail, try/fail, try/fail, cry approach you've likely used for your presentations so far.

We've suffered from years of being told a random set of wildly misleading rules in presentations – such as don't use more than ten words per page; don't use more than twenty slides; make your presentation this many minutes long. You must do this, must do that. These rules give a sense of certainty and are attractive because they seem to make things easy, but they are inflexible, hard to adapt and don't cater for your individual circumstances, so they aren't serving you well.

Your experience and the scenario of your presentation's context is unique, and most of these rules are really just someone else's opinion. They lack a proper explanation or science behind them, and what works for one industry or audience may not work for you. I've seen the consequences of people following rigid rules in their presentation yet missing vital elements that cause a devastating lack of impact.

So, I'm not going to give you rules. Instead, what I'll offer you is a way of thinking and a process that I know works. I'll encourage you to think about what you can apply from this to your own presentations. These are suggestions, so take what you like and ignore what you don't. If something works for you, go for it, even if I've said otherwise. Let's get started.

Know what you want

If any other business process performed as inefficiently as this, it would be thrown out, deleted or given notice. So, why is the corporate workhorse – the thirty-to-sixty-minute business PowerPoint presentation – still around? Why are we still sitting in our seats, watching slide after slide, desperately hoping for the experience to end so we can clap politely, grab the handout, and – with a sense of relief – move on to something else? Why aren't we calling these experiences out as wasteful: of our time, energy and focus? In an era when our most precious commodity is time, why aren't we actively defending it? Where's the transformation?

There are two situations I can think of that involve a group of people sitting still in complete silence while one person is talking and has all the attention. The first is live comedy: an event when a (hopefully!) skilled, engaging comedian attempts to show a group of people a new perspective on something they haven't seen before. They use timing, wit, energy and contrast to insert something into our minds that's so different it makes us laugh. It's beautiful. If you've seen a master practitioner like Bill Burr, Hannah Gadsby or Dave Chappelle in action, it's an art form that makes an impact. You can see the work they've put in and the effect it's had.

While you've got that image of humour and artistry in your head, let's contrast that with the second situation: the formal corporate business presentation with the accompanying forty-two-slide deck.

How does that feel in comparison? Urgh. Yuck... Right? If your experience has been anything like that of most adult professionals, you're likely to recall a heavy, sinking, out-of-body experience that your imagination tries to force you away from even thinking about. Whether it's a conference, staff town hall meeting, sales pitch, workshop or professional development day, a lot of them suck. Slide after slide of 'blah, blah, blah, click' content full of self-interest and muddled thoughts, with some clipart thrown in.

Not all comedy shows are great, and not all corporate presentations are terrible, but I think it's fair to say that on average, one is a far better experience for the audience than the other. In comedy, the outcome the comedian wants is to make you laugh. It's a hard job to do but has an easily defined, singular objective of *what they want from you.*

This is the key. The starting point in becoming a better presenter is that when it's time to present, you know what the change is that you want to take place in your audience. Ask yourself, 'What do I want the future to look like after I present?'

Think about the last presentation you attended. Take a moment. Can you explain what the presenter wanted from you in one sentence? What part of your future did they want to change? If your experience is like most, I'm going to guess you can't answer that. I'm also going to say that the presenter couldn't, either!

Why should the audience listen to you?

In both of the scenarios above, the interaction is an exchange: the audience gives their time and attention, and in return, the presenter/comedian attempts to give them something that benefits them.

For a comedian to get their outcome, they write, rehearse, take a risk and work hard. In a business presentation, most of the time the exchange isn't fair for the audience. We tend to slap content together, read straight from our dull slides, and then ask something of our audience that might involve complex decision-making, be expensive or mean a change in their behaviour.

We ask them to take a risk and to trust us. We ask for people's time and then want them to do hard, complicated things on top of that. It's not a fair exchange. Contrast how hard a comedian is working for a simple laugh with what is at stake in your presentation and how hard you're trying to get it.

How did we get to such an unfair place? I was eager to know. Throughout a five-year period of running presentation workshops for groups, I'd open each session with the same question to attendees: I'd ask them to think back to a recent presentation they'd sat through, and which details they could recall.

I've probably asked that question to, and received replies from, over 3,000 people. It quickly became my unofficial survey. By asking a broad and diverse group, I was trying to gain a better insight into the common aspects of presentations that were making an impact and actually connecting with audiences. I wanted to know what really stuck days, weeks or even years after the event.

Everyone was free to respond genuinely. I wasn't their manager or team member asking them; I was an independent observer asking them on the spot without notice. Almost everyone I asked really struggled to recall a single example and reply. Despite having been the victims of hundreds of business presentations, it was always a challenging task for them to remember one on the spot. They'd had plenty of experience attending all types of presentations, but almost all of them had been unmemorable. A very small group with good memories were able to recall a specific presentation, but this was usually limited to a rough idea of the presentation and some basic factual details.

An even smaller group were able to recall a presentation positively and accurately. What's more, they had understood what the presenter was trying to achieve. What was fascinating was watching the process of their recollection. Even years later, the first part of what they'd recall was how they felt about the presentation, then they were able to recall the main message, and then with a bit more time, the details would come back to them. What they'd seen had had an impact. It was still with them. Some change had happened.

Through this informal research, I was amazed to see a wide variance in the impact that thirty to forty-five minutes of a shared presentation time can have. From 'delete after attending' to life-changing. If presentations are a part of your role, this should be a sobering insight into how most presentations just happen and are forgotten; very few cut through.

Every time you present, you are given an opportunity to do something amazing, whatever the topic. It can be frustrating and hard work and you may suffer setbacks, but this should be your lightbulb moment. You can change the future and I'll show you how.

Just to note

We've all been the victims of presentations we can't even remember. Today is the day you can take the first step towards changing that. It won't be immediate, but every improvement you make will take you towards leaving a lasting impact on your audience. From now on, your presentations will have an objective, a mission. Let's go and achieve that.

2
Making An Impact

I'm not here to coddle you and tell you that none of this is your fault. After all, you are the only person who can transform the way you present. But there are a lot of valid reasons why you've got to this point...

Why most presentations suck

If you are working in a large organisation, you may have seen a CEO, board member or senior executive present, or you may have been to a conference and seen a keynote speaker and thought, 'Wow, that's not bad, I'd like to be that type of presenter.' Unfortunately, these high-level presenters possess an unfair advantage over you that you can't easily overcome. At the top level of business, these presenters are highly experienced as they've been around for a long time and have had the chance to practise delivery hundreds, if not thousands, of times.

When the stakes are high and the value of winning or losing is clear, they also have more resources at their disposal and, often, a whole team supporting them. With so much on the line, they make significant investments in coaching and assistance to fine-tune their presentations. McKinsey consultants are taught The McKinsey Way of structuring and developing a presentation and it's pretty good. BCG and Deloitte all have their own, equally interesting and effective approaches. Presentation Design Co may have even worked with them behind the scenes to create something amazing!

If you aren't in that privileged position of having a team to work with you, you're left to grind it out by yourself without the same level of experience or support. When the need to present arises, you are at a huge disadvantage as you are working solo, especially if you are starting from scratch in a new product, service or role. If you've been there, you'll know how hard it is to know exactly what you need to do to make an impact. If you aren't lucky enough to be trained at length in a proprietary process, it's easy to feel lost and not know what to do.

In the hunt for inspiration and guidance, it's natural to look at great presenters for guidance. Steve Jobs is a starting point and the TED library is full of beautiful presentations. TED Talks are powerful, embracing and great models for us to be inspired by, but they are often only narrow types of presentations with a fixed time limit, significant production value and, generally, a highly engaged audience. This is quite different to the style and setting that you and most business presenters will face. They serve as aspirational, motivational examples but they are far too big a jump for most presenters to model themselves on and follow for their own presentations.

In a typical presentation scenario when you are under pressure and short on time, there is a bias towards working on the visible, tangible components of a presentation. This might look like opening an existing PowerPoint (once you've finished checking your emails again), writing a new title, getting to an agenda slide and starting to fill out the content. The natural tendency to 'just get going' is a symptom of not knowing where to start and what to do. We all know where that ends up.

Developing a presentation can feel like a cumbersome task and the immediate payoff isn't as strong as the eight other things landing on our list for the day. It's a creative, thinking process at odds with some of the short-term tasks that need to be done.

If someone comes past and finds you staring out of the window, deeply considering the challenge ahead and the needs of the audience, it's not as convincing as if you're up to slide thirty-two, inserting graphs and bashing away at the computer looking like you're almost there.

So, what happens? It's likely that you push it down your list of priorities. Like an assignment, your presentation can start with great intentions and lofty goals that ultimately morph into a deadline-driven, fear-induced panic that feels like an enormous weight hanging over you.

At the same time, when you sit (or hopefully stand) in front of your computer, you are faced with a constant distraction, as the tool that we use to create our presentations is the same one we use for messaging, collaboration and meetings. Being at your desk looking at the calendar of things that need to be addressed and then seeing the presentation you have scheduled in two weeks' time can create a sense of anxiety as you hack through slides trying to make progress to throw a 'presso' together.

It's a common scenario that is taking place across businesses right now. Highly skilled, experienced people under time pressure, trudging through Google images and trying to arrange smart art diagrams to match what's in their head and what they are trying to communicate. They are trying their best but, despite their efforts, will ultimately miss the mark. This just isn't a path to a presentation that makes an impact, it's most likely going to suck.

If you take a moment to think about it, the pressure that people put themselves under by not having a reliable and proven process to make a presentation is crazy. It's also avoidable. There is hope.

The ugly elephant that crept into the room

If we think back over the last ten years or so, changes in the business applications we use, the introduction of new ones and advancements in the power of hardware have been transformational, to say the least. We've successfully moved on from the iPhone 4 and Windows 8. Uber isn't just for a ride to the airport. Our data has magically moved from a server room to the cloud and generative AI is transforming our working lives.

Let's talk about PowerPoint – a true visual aid. Used by over 85% of presenters in business, PowerPoint has its roots back in 35mm slide projectors. Slides were expensive to make, required thought and were a fun 1970s way to share your Italian holiday with friends, maybe over a fondue, listening to Cher while drinking a lovely Chablis. That's the image I have in my head at least – it was a bit before my time!

As technology evolved and we started to use visual aids in our presentations, the tools were either overhead projectors or printed slides created by the art department. Again, high costs and specialist skills were involved. Memos and reports were being prepared by centralised typing pools.

With the launch of Microsoft Office in 1997 and office applications, suddenly there was a way to reduce the cost and increase the speed of creating presentations – everyone could now do it themselves. And that's where things started to go really wrong.

PowerPoint slowly crept into the role of a business presenter. It didn't announce itself with a big bang, it just kind of appeared and has now become pervasive. But there was a fundamental problem: PowerPoint was a software designed to address business problems with technology, not a solution to a communication problem. There was no mass movement calling out for chequerboard transitions. There wasn't a popular petition calling out for more of the ability to make 3D clipart bounce around the screen. These features were built in as novelty features that came in over the top to make up for the fact that most people aren't great at designing slides. It's not core to their job or skillset, but they've been given the task of making their presentations interesting, so it's really tempting to add in some fluff.

With the rollout of Microsoft Office to the corporate world, all the unique variables of a business presentation became standardised. Without us realising it,

PowerPoint and presentations became intertwined. The quality of presentations suffered, as what it took to create a great PowerPoint wasn't what it took to create a great presentation.

Rather than first defining audiences and objectives and thinking at a high level, we now think of our starting point for a presentation as building an agenda and filling out slides. This process of trying to force all presentations into a 16:9 slide template with an agenda and 12pt Arial font has made most presentations suck. Big, complex ideas become relegated to bullet points. Insights and ideas that need time to digest get stuck on twelve slides. And the way that we think and reflect on information is sacrificed to the needs of a formatted deck, where making sure your logo on each slide is important to tick the branding box. As General McMaster says, 'It's dangerous because it can create the illusion of understanding and the illusion of control – some problems in the world are not bullet-isable.'

And so, 'Death by PowerPoint' was born. Over time, we've decided to accept the horrible collective experience of sitting through a poorly developed presentation, but it doesn't take much for us to disengage. Just a couple of bad slides in with a monotone presenter brings up memories of dozens of past dull presentations, and we decide early on that we're out. You can almost hear the audience thinking, 'We know what's coming,' and you don't even stand a chance. They sit through your presentation accepting that, 'It is what it is,' while underneath the surface, they feel frustrated and silently object by disengaging.

Overcoming 'PowerPoint first' thinking

Jeff Bezos, Elon Musk and Steve Jobs were CEOs that all famously banned PowerPoint presentations at some point. Jeff would get people to write out long-form ideas and submit them before a meeting – he wanted people to think deeper and clearer. Steve was short on patience and wanted people to communicate quickly and effectively so that more time was left for discussion and interrogation. If you want to make an impact, overcoming this 'PowerPoint first' thinking is one of the first, most powerful steps you need to take. Luckily, it's an easy one. I'll show you how.

What do presenters and Navy SEALs have in common?

Imagine a group of professionally trained US Navy SEALs on the ground, looking to develop and present the latest high-stakes strategy. What do you imagine it looks like when elite performers with high stakes prepare to present a mission? Do you imagine them arguing over what font they should use for PowerPoint?

This should be a joke, but sadly, it's not. That's exactly what happens. When it comes to PowerPoint, both you and a seasoned Navy SEAL are ready to smash that keyboard in despair at the exact same moment. Here's a direct quote from decorated Navy SEAL Andy Stumpf: 'Our normal planning cycle was 24–72 hours sitting in front of PowerPoint ... arguing over the font that we're using to submit for mission approval.' Speaking on the *Joe Rogan Experience* podcast, Andy revealed his true frustrations of having to use PowerPoint for life-or-death strategies. In fact, his team's issues with PowerPoint were so severe that they seriously affected their day-to-day operations: 'If you wanted to shut down the average-day military, it wouldn't be through a kinetic act. You would need to put some type of code into Microsoft Office – and we're done.' Your irritated sighs as you struggle to right align your text in your agenda slide don't seem so crazy anymore, do they?

The Navy SEAL issue is an equally comical and insane scenario. PowerPoint is a problem that's endemic across businesses, governments, educational institutions and teams, both large and small. It's frustrating and doesn't stack up from a business perspective, either. In reality:

Hours of Work × Frustration Weighting
+ Other Stuff You Should Have Done
= The Real Cost of Your Time in PowerPoint

Thinking in slides hides real thinking

When I started Presentation Design Co, we initially specialised in creating Prezi presentations. If you haven't seen Prezi, instead of using slides, it's a big, open canvas that allows you to zoom in and out of content in a non-linear way. It can look amazing, and clients were very excited to step outside the constraints of slides and start to give their presentation movement using the zoom feature of Prezi.

The starting point of planning a Prezi was to first develop the 'big picture' theme that the presentation would explore. We'd then set out the framework for the groups of content before creating the content inside of those groups. To make sure the Prezi flowed smoothly and didn't jump around too much (or people started to feel sick!), we needed to have a really well-organised presentation flow. To do this, we had a huge whiteboard installed in our office. With a marker in hand, we worked with clients to map out the structure and content of their presentation one building block at a time.

As we worked in Prezi every day, for us, it felt that this first straightforward step of organising content into a flow should be a pretty simple task. These presenters were often experienced in business and knew the details of what they wanted to speak about. How wrong we were. It was often a painstaking process to define even a basic structure with them, as they would jump into the minor points or content details and struggled to really draw out a big picture about how their presentation would flow.

Years of working in slides had ruined their ability to get perspective and to see 'all' of their presentation – how things should fit together outside of slides to create a flow and make an impact. The record still stands at a day-and-a-half of working with a client just to get to that first step. It wasn't time wasted though. That time included discussion, thought and debate that led to a more effective presentation. They were seeing things with a fresh perspective and able to think outside of slides. It was worth it in the end, but that didn't make it any less painful to work through.

I've been through this process of interrogating and exploring the fundamentals of a presentation hundreds of times. I've covered almost every type of presentation and industry and seen just how prevalent 'slide thinking' is. It's given me a true insight to just how much it holds us back from making an impact.

PowerPoint doesn't need a process to create slides, but you will need to use one to create a good presentation. Everyone has been drawn into slide thinking for so long, it's hard to imagine anything different. For too long we've been focusing on creating slides without first creating the foundational structure.

Just to note

Slide thinking is a trap, but it's one you can get out of. So let me offer you a way to do something different. To no longer suck. The ability to truly make an impact even when you use PowerPoint. Let me help you change the future.

3
Win The War
For Attention

People are busy. And busy people make snap decisions and snap judgements. People will make them about you. And I'll tell you how you can be OK with it – because you have to be.

People won't let you waste their time

The world of business is dynamic and continually changing. So are the lives of the audiences that you present to. Dramatically. We now live in the 'attention economy' where there's a surplus of content for us to devour as we please. A real-life war is being waged for their attention. After all, it's a valuable commodity and there's a huge group of platforms and businesses trying intensely hard to capture it.

What would have been successful just ten years ago isn't any longer. To make an impact when you present, the bar required to keep and hold an audience's attention has been raised significantly. *You are in a war for your audience's attention.* You need to acknowledge this shift, and you need to win.

Behind closed doors, executives and communications teams share the unvarnished truth with us of the despair they feel about how poorly their presenters are performing in this war. They share how they see people who are capable in their role but can't present well enough to keep an audience's attention, and how losing this war is having terrible consequences for their business.

Clients have also shared the desperate ways they've tried to overcome these issues. One was the head of a huge sales team who had no faith left in her team's ability to execute. She kept control of their presentations by using word-for-word, pre-approved presentation scripts and locking the editing on their slide decks.

I remember the utter frustration of a marketing team at all the hard work and money they'd put into an all-staff town hall, only to have an unprepared CEO stand up and spend twenty-five minutes free-styling and waffling. Needless to say, they destroyed any sense of engagement or excitement with the amateur approach at odds with the preparation of the team supporting them.

Clarity on your role as a presenter

To win the war for attention, you first need to get clarity on your role as a presenter and understand a few hard truths on the steps you need to take.

1. You are going to be judged

At that moment, you have a window of opportunity to connect and engage with an audience, move them to a different perspective and influence their thinking. The window you must do this in closes rapidly; if you miss it then you are seldom guaranteed a second chance to change the future. To make this even harder, whether you like it or not, you're also being judged when you present – and probably a lot more than you're comfortable with. This may not be a pleasant feeling, but to win the war, you need to be aware of this and get used to it. Don't shy away from it.

This is hard as in our professional roles, we typically receive judgement from others in longer-term metrics with clear criteria, for example, whether you've reached your sales target, your 360 feedback results or your manager choosing a rating in your performance review. In a presentation, you step away from your computer into a live environment where, as the centre of attention, your audience is making snap judgements about how you look, your ideas, your delivery style, your voice, your slide design – all these things and more. It's the uncomfortable world of performance in which actors, musicians and social media influencers live.

Having so much at stake when presenting and going through the process of being judged can feel like a crippling challenge but accept this as part of the experience. Know that if you can survive this and thrive, the rewards are high.

2. That judgement is going to take place over three stages

The first is the initial snap judgement – the first impression. We've all heard that it's seven seconds, but it's not. In fact, *you've got just one second* before your audience makes a snap judgement about whether they know, trust or like you and there's very little you can do to influence this first impression.

The second judgement is during the next 30–40 seconds after you start presenting. This is the chance for the audience to stop and make a deeper, more informed judgement. The good news is that *this second impression is entirely in your control* and it's why this part of your presentation is critically important to get right.

The third impression is at the end of your presentation when you wrap things up. This is really a summary of how you've finished and an overall impression of how you've done.

Understanding and accepting these judgements and knowing that you can influence them will hugely assist you in the battle.

3. You need to be a performer

When you spend a large proportion of your time in meetings, conversations and groups engaging in synchronous communication, what does it feel like when it's time to get up in front of people and watch your audience be quiet and (hopefully) give you their attention? For most of us, it just doesn't feel comfortable. A very small group of people are born performers and when that moment they've been waiting for comes, they can flick the switch and be utterly at ease in front of a live audience. For most of us though, it's the opposite. It's a nerve-inducing, fearful act. It keeps us up at night for days and weeks beforehand. We run through terrible scenarios in our heads of all the disasters that could happen. Our confidence hits the floor.

When comedians perform, they have the advantage of their audience being on a night out and even having had a drink or two, or they may well be a couple in themselves. In the sober world of business, when it comes to presenting, we've got so many things running through our minds that act as a barrier. It may be nerves, worrying about the audience's reaction or running late. You may be thinking, 'What will I look like? Am I saying things to keep my boss happy? Is what I'm saying even correct?' If the presentation is online, will everyone be able to hear the building work next door or a bunch of noisy kids?

It's a huge challenge to maintain the poise needed to present well, but presenters that can accept and embrace that it's part of what's required are much better positioned to win the war. To be effective, we need to be present, confident, polished and engaged with the people we address. It isn't easy to be yourself when you're stood in front of a screen presenting. It's hard to make a genuine connection when you're sat talking to a webcam. It often can feel just a bit off and that makes the challenge that much harder.

Have you ever had a conversation with a presenter after they've spoken and felt you've got more from that interaction than their presentation? Or have you noticed the energy change at the end of a slide deck when someone gets asked a question and, without knowing, switches to a more natural, comfortable, interesting version of themselves when talking? This is the energy you want to harness for your own presentations. Relaxed, personable and relatable.

4. You can change the future

You *should* change the future. It doesn't matter where you sit in the hierarchy, or what you've done to date. I believe you can be that person who creates something that has such an impact that months or years later, your message isn't forgotten. People will be able to recall what they've heard you say and you will have played some role in affecting their lives.

A bad presentation is like watching a car crash in slow motion and you're hopeless to help out in any way, shape or form. These clients are forced to give their team members and leaders some not-so-truthful feedback at the end. You could easily think that this is just a localised problem. Maybe presentations aren't meant to be any better and we just need to accept our inevitable death by PowerPoint.

But I can't stand for this. Because it isn't just about presentations; it is much bigger than that. If we look ahead, as a group of people, we collectively have some monumental, generational, mission-critical problems we need to come together to solve.

We need better energy solutions to fix a damaged climate, we need to resolve structural unfairness and remove the constraints of inequality, and we need to make massive shifts in how we provide healthcare and education while looking for peaceful solutions for our geo-political tensions.

We need this against a backdrop of the rate of change increasing. Technology will change. Our corporate structures will develop. We may move from fiat currency to crypto and blockchain. AI will play an intricate part in our daily lives and our world will change.

Despite all of this, it's communication between people that will allow us to mobilise and make change happen. Leaders will speak and move their teams to action, salespeople will bring great products to customers, trainers will offer us better ways to do things and educators will show us not what to think, but how to gather wisdom. We need to cut through and find a better way.

This will happen one presentation at a time. There are pieces of the puzzle – millions of them – all addressing problems in their own way. To date, our collective approach and effectiveness have been largely holding us back. We can – we must – get better at doing this. We need to *stop* going through the motions and *start* deciding to make an impact. It's time for us all to sharpen our skills and do better, not because we should, but because we have to.

The good news is that, with some guidance, any presenter can improve. *You* can start to improve the next time you present. It's a stressful, tough job to prepare a presentation, and it can be lonely when you're up in front of a group. You might be scared to set a goal of improving to become a great presenter. Yes, it can be one of the greatest fears, but any big challenge comes with a massive reward when you face it and succeed.

The starting point of this is the foundational ability that determines whether your audience pays attention and if you can generate a positive judgement (or not). The great news is that with the right mindset and process, you can develop this foundation very quickly, even if you have fallen short in the past.

I want you to be proud of what you do; I want you to feel confident you're progressing. If you've ever felt the buzz of nailing it, you know this is one of the best feelings in the world. I've witnessed it in the faces, voices and excited post-presentation emails of clients who've had that breakthrough and finally achieved that result. It's the feeling of satisfaction and the reward of making an impact.

Just to note

Making a difference with your presentations isn't easy, but it will be worthwhile, I promise. I am going to take you through my 5 Power Principles and our 4D presentation process and give you the answers. Let's get started.

PART TWO
THE 5 POWER PRINCIPLES

F ed up with delivering snooze fest presentations? Ready to enjoy finally making an impact? The secret is that all the magic happens before you even make your first slide. The real starting point is your mindset: how you approach thinking about your presentation will give you a wildly different outcome.

There are five, easy to follow, easy to implement power principles that are going to separate you from the rest of the average presenters and make you one of the best.

4
Power Principle #1: The Audience Is Number One

You'll only get to make an impact with your audience if you make your presentation about them. It's as simple as that.

People don't care what's in it for you

The first step to becoming a better presenter isn't about learning or doing something new. It's not a technique or a hack. When there are burning holes in almost every presentation, giving you quick fixes might make sense. But at this stage, giving you something new would be akin to filling a bucket before repairing the hole in its side.

Instead, what I strongly suggest – *no, plead with you to do* – is focus on transforming and removing the biggest weakness and number one source of failure I see in most presentations: not focusing on the needs of your audience.

I've seen charming, smart presenters practise for hours with stunning decks – and yet set themselves up for failure and destroy their chances of making an impact when they ignore this fundamental principle.

While there are many practical ways to improve, this principle needs to be a cornerstone for everything. Engagement, delivery and confidence are important elements of success, but making sure you understand the needs of your audience and create your presentation to address them, is so important it almost goes beyond being a principle.

It should be seen as a mindset, a guide, a North Star embedded in everything you do. It's such a simple principle that you might be thinking, 'Kris, isn't this a little obvious?' Yes, it is obvious! And so, riddle me this: even though it's so important and obvious, why is it consistently overlooked in most presentations? *Sigh* On we go.

Most of a presentation is a solo process

The origin of not prioritising the needs of your audience has its roots in the context of the presentation development and design process generally being a solo act. A presentation starts in our head. We might consult people to help form its content, but most of the time, it's a solitary act, where our audience doesn't have much of a presence.

During this solitary process, we work on sales presentations where we want people to buy something, so we focus on selling. We create workshops where we want to share content with attendees; we plan forums where we want to update staff on our results and what's happening. We run client functions to launch new products and keep them updated. We take them through a new platform. We spend a lot of time thinking about what we have to say and what we need to 'cover'.

With this internal focus, it's completely understandable that you can be blinded by your own internal focus and create presentations where the ideas and content miss the opportunity to fulfil your audience's needs – and so you fail to make the impact needed.

So, how do you immediately start to move from where you are to where you can make the audience number one? You pledge to stop thinking about you. Instead, set yourself a mission to become a dedicated, humble servant to your audience's needs. In this new role, you're committing to always understand their needs, thoughts and feelings: your presentation will answer, guide, inform, influence and change them. You pledge to be there for them, not you.

The amazing thing is you can make this commitment now, before finishing this page. It costs nothing and takes no time, but you'll start to enjoy the benefits almost immediately. All you need to do is say, 'I am there for my audience.' Go for it. Do this now. Say out loud, 'I am a humble servant there to meet the needs of my audience.'

How does that feel? You are already on your way to enjoying a massive transformation to a high-impact presenter and improving every presentation you will ever make.

I've already mentioned the idea that in a presentation, an exchange occurs between the presenter and the audience. In most business presentations, most of the time, the presenter doesn't deliver enough. It's not fair. If you've made the pledge to put your audience as number 1, look back at the last presentation you gave (or the last one you attended). Now ask yourself:

- Who benefitted from it?
- Was the presenter really there for the audience?
- Was it obvious?
- Whose needs were being met?

If you were lucky enough to have watched a humble servant as a presenter, they will surely stand out. If your last presentation didn't deliver on this pledge, what role did the presenter assume instead? What is the opposite of the humble servant? The self-focused salesperson? The wavering waffler? The know-it-all rambler? The conceited CEO? The ego-driven executive?

As humans, we are always looking for new ideas and ways of thinking that make life easier. We want our problems solved and fewer things that burden us. We're open and welcoming to those who share these with us. If you aren't a humble servant when presenting, you aren't serving us, you're taking away our attention and distracting us from our mission. You are making life harder.

I work with clients to take on this principle and I've seen when that lightbulb moment clicks with them. When they take on this new mindset. As soon as it happens, they look back at their earlier presentations and start seeing the gaps their old thinking created. They suddenly understand why they didn't make an impact. With this principle embedded, it starts to feel obvious and instantly gives them a new way to approach their presentations.

Don't be a bad party guest

When I made this shift in mindset, I then was able to better reflect on my early days working in banking and the type of presentations I gave. I also started to feel a great sense of awkwardness and let-down at just how badly not putting the needs of my audience first had stopped me from making an impact.

Many years ago, the bank I was working for launched a structured income product for financial advisors. It was new and a bit more complex than other products available to them at the time. As a salesperson, I was given a presentation spot to help promote it at the professional development day of a big group of advisors.

A week before marketing sent me the deck, I had memorised the notes and felt fully prepared to talk to the group about how great our product was, how well it was going to work and why we were so great.

Can you see the problem? It's obvious now, isn't it?

It only took about nine slides before I knew I had lost most of the group. It was a horrible experience to plough through the rest, and I left feeling devastated. I thought I had done OK with the delivery but felt uneasy not knowing why I'd failed so badly and had even had a semi-hostile response.

In the post-debrief with the team, we arrogantly decided that it was probably due to the product being too complex for the group to comprehend in forty-five minutes. It wasn't. There were people in that room far smarter and more experienced than me. They could grasp financial concepts in an instant. They just didn't engage with another speaker taking forty-five minutes to tell them how great something was so they'd recommend it to their clients. It wasn't a fair exchange.

At the time, all I was interested in was my needs and my presentation. It's like those awful conversations at parties when someone takes over – it's all one way, all about them. In a small group, it's obnoxious; in a presentation, it's awful.

If I could turn back time, I'd ditch the slides and take a couple of days to think, reflect and even reach out to a couple of audience members to ask questions and understand their thinking. I would then be ultra-clear in my presentation about what I could do to assist as their humble servant. What were the problems in their business that truly concerned them; where did this product sit; what was the bridge; how could I help them? Advisors may well have been interested in the product, but without this mindset, I'd never find my way to truly help them and create a successful outcome.

In the rush, it's easy to assume. That's also a safe option. When you have a presentation coming up, ask yourself these questions:

- How can I serve the needs of the audience I speak to?

- What are their problems?

- What worries them?

- What are their biases?

- What am I doing to help them?

- How will I make this a fair exchange?

You can do this through an email, meeting, LinkedIn poll survey or even online with a tool like answerthe-public.com.

Start asking these questions before you create any-thing, or if you are already on the path, go and interro-gate what you've already done using this perspective as your new lens. Bring this principle into your think-ing and I guarantee it will start to transform your ideas, your content, the words you use, what you put on your slides and your outcome. It will reduce your nerves and balance your mindset to a more natural way of thinking.

Presentations are unique in that every presenter has had the experience of being an audience member on the receiving end of a presentation. That gives them both perspectives to reflect on this principle and eval-uate it. 'But I need something from them!' you shout. Sure you do, and that's OK. You've got a sale to make, investors to convince, minds to change. But to make an impact, all that must come second.

Whatever your needs are, to be truly successful in get-ting there with the highest outcome, you need to align with the audience's needs. If you can't, either keep working to find a way or don't do it at all. Don't turn up to waste their time and yours.

One of the sentences I most hate to hear from clients is, 'We need to tell them about X without any reference to the Why.' Your presentation isn't a brochure. Google knows more than you do. When we aren't our audience's humble servant, it's easy to get stuck in arrogance and talk about problems instead of solving them.

We're sick of being yelled at and sold to. In the normal course of the day, we're dealing with billboards, Facebook ads, pop-ups and sponsored content. Our skills at blocking these out are phenomenal; your audience will put up this same barrier to block you out if they think you aren't there for them.

Using the word 'servant' may trigger you. Egos are involved. But it's critical to move past this. One of the less helpful techniques we've been told to use to deal with nerves is to 'puff out our chests' and prove ourselves with inflated confidence. Trust me, this one isn't helpful. In fact, it often only elevates the ego's importance. Confidence is important, but a huge ego is holding you back.

As an audience member, how would you feel if you were watching a presenter who was truly there for you? Tuned in to your needs, wants, fears and questions? How much more likely are you to respond to their message, take the next step with them or genuinely want to ask them a meaningful question?

Four steps to transform into a humble servant

Here are four easy steps to help you in the process of transforming your mindset from self-focused to making the audience your priority.

1. **Ask questions to understand your audience's needs.** Become an expert in their problems. Dive in. Speak directly to them. If you can't speak to them, then think about them. What's important to them? What are their fears and drivers; what do they know; what are their knowledge gaps? Talk, engage, post on LinkedIn, do whatever you need to do to ask the questions you need answers for. It's very easy to assume we know these things already, but the power of continuously following this step will keep you close, relevant and allow you to best serve them.

2. **Work out how to best address them.** Use the needs you identified in Step 1 as the base for this step. Which ones are you solving? It might not be possible to solve all of them, so don't overextend the scope of what you're offering. Instead, focus on how your solution addresses the needs it does solve. As part of this, you may be asking your audience to change their way of thinking.

What is that new way, and how can they bridge the gap between it and where they are now? Work out how to guide your audience to the conclusion you want them to reach. Hopefully, that's one that shows them how you can address their needs. This shows you're on their side.

3. **Prove you can solve them.** If you know what your audience's needs are and can meet those needs, show you can do so in a credible and effective way. It's not about telling people what you can do, it's about *showing* them. Use case studies, stories and products. Build people's confidence to follow you, to believe you and to be open to your ideas. This builds a commonality and shared purpose.

4. **Don't assume people know your solution.** Imagine you're a novice at whatever topic your presentation is on. View your content through a fresh set of objective eyes. Ask yourself:

   - How much of your content has a prerequisite understanding that everyone listening to you might not have?

   - Is there anything that you are addressing that needs a prior explanation?

   - What assumptions have you set in place about your audience? Have you communicated this?

   - Are you taking the steps to make sure that you've eliminated the obstacles for an audience to understand?

- When it comes down to it, are you sure your presentation would make sense to everyone listening?

By following these four steps, you are making a genuine commitment to being a humble servant. You'll begin to transform your approach and the flow of your presentation. You now live in your audience's world – you can think like them, you can connect and you can better make an impact.

Still stuck? That's OK. The following practical examples demonstrate what the shift in mindset looks like. As you read them, put yourself in the audience's shoes. What's the difference you feel between the 'self-focused' and 'humble servant' statements? These should allow you to go back and examine your own presentation in the same way.

Example 1: The sales pitch

Self-focused: I want them to know we're the best platform insurance product in the market – far better than our competitor's. We can do x, y and z that they can't, and that makes our product 20% better than them. Ready to buy it?

Humble servant: My audience's main problem is they have legacy systems, but their team are very experienced in Band-Aids and manual workarounds, so they have a comfort and familiarity with the status quo.

However, the speed of processing customer claims is costing them money and reputational damage.

There are three ways we've been able to support similar businesses to transition to our platform. The result has been a two-thirds reduction in complaints, and half the write-offs.

Example 2: The investment pitch

Self-focused: Here's what we're doing and here's what we need money for. With it, we're going to do x, y and z (ie, all these clever ideas I have).

Humble servant: I trust that you recognise plenty of good opportunities. Here's why you can trust me with your money, and here's what we've embedded into the offer that makes our investors a priority.

Example 3: The team presentation

Self-focused: The broader business needs to better understand what our team does and why we're important. Here are a bunch of things I want them to know about what we bring to the company.

Humble servant: As a business, embracing a customer experience approach is how we will compete and win. We have a shared goal of improving the current customer experience. Here's what our team can offer you to improve how we work together to make this happen faster, and with better results.

Start with the magic word

If you're out of time and can't get to the deep thinking you need to do to restructure what you're presenting, or you're looking for an easy place to start, here's another simple way: use 'with' instead of 'to'.

When you're looking at your content, slides and notes, any time you see the word 'to', strike it out. Do your best to use the word 'with'. It's not just a powerful word; it's a catalyst for better framing what you're delivering as a shared experience and creating a greater impact. Often, you'll change the way you say things to make 'with' fit, and you'll end up expressing yourself in a more connecting, engaging way.

Consider how it feels to hear things like, 'I'm here to speak to you about...' versus, 'I'm here to share with you...'

'With' is a single, powerful word that changes your thinking. It helps to develop a giving mindset. Be there for your audience. Don't hold back.

CASE STUDY: Avoid the trap of being an expert

Glen Carlson is the co-founder of Dent Global, a training and consulting company helping entrepreneurs scale up, and making their businesses stand out.

With a strong background in events, consulting, training and running successful businesses himself – and doing the same for hundreds of other businesses – he's a well-qualified, recognised expert in his field.

With this significant set of accomplishments, he could easily work on the commonly seen, 'Trust me; I'm an expert,' approach to crafting his presentations, but he doesn't.

What sets Glen apart is his mastery of the art of making his audience the centre of everything he does. He presents on video and at conferences, events and training sessions with a laser focus on solving problems for his audience. He knows his audience and he speaks directly to them, aligning his words, delivery and communication structure accordingly. You don't just know that he's there for his audience, you can *feel* it. He isn't wasting your time. He's there for you.

This approach is completely genuine and by speaking via his passion, Glen doesn't need to be perfectly polished. With his problem-solving mindset, he comes across as personable, authentic, relatable, knowledgeable and real.

When you speak to a shared problem, you immediately become much more interesting to your audience. What's the natural next step people look for after a problem? A solution. Speak to your audience's problems and you'll capture their energy, interest and support as you share how you can help solve them.

As an expert, there are different approaches Glen could take. It'd be easy to follow a self-focused path of 'opinion' that only shares his perspective on the 'why'. He could have a mindset of showing people they're wrong, but he doesn't.

He knows the business and entrepreneurship world is filled with problems and to make an impact, he needs to meet his audience there. He fulfils the role of serving their needs. Watch a video of Glen presenting at www.dent.global and then consider the following questions:

- What did you see that stands out?

- How did the presentation make you feel?

- What can you model from seeing Glen present?

- What's the most important thing to *your* audience?

Understand and speak to that, then use it to frame your content.

Self-assessment and reflection

Now it's time to reflect on where you are as a humble servant using a simple ranking. Score yourself on the following criteria, being as honest as you can with a score out of ten:

- As a presenter, I'm proactively polling, questioning and reaching out to my target audience to accurately understand their needs. __ / 10

- I use language in my presentation that demonstrates I'm there for my audience. __ / 10

- I share examples and case studies to demonstrate that I'm there for my audience. __ / 10

- I'm mindful of removing my ego and the self-centred parts of my presentation. __ / 10

- I feel my presentation represents a fair exchange for my audience. __ / 10

Reflect on your scores and then decide on three specific actions you can take to demonstrate a humble servant mindset in your next presentation. Make a note of these and be sure to use them.

Just to note

The mindset shift to go from serving yourself to your audience is, in theory, a simple one. But it's also a game-changer, one that opens you up to not only the possibility of a better version of yourself, but also the success and positivity this generates. It's a win-win situation, and you're now one step closer to achieving it.

5

Power Principle #2: Start With The End In Mind

You want your presentation to have an impact, right? What impact? What specific action do you want your audience to take after your presentation? This will guide everything that follows.

Every presentation is a journey

Even though you have an audience to serve, you still want something from them. It could just be an open mind to your way of thinking, or it could be action, investment or a sale. Whatever it is, you need to be crystal clear on what the end goal of the presentation looks like.

Only once you have that clarity can you start to create a journey for your audience – from before your presentation to their changed state after it. Looking back at the closing moments of your last presentation, what were your final words? How did you make your audience feel? What was the interaction immediately after you finished presenting? What happened in your moment of truth?

Did you read off the slides until you got to, 'Any questions?' where you waited, hoping, wishing, praying for a rapturous round of applause or an interested query? Did you get what you wanted or were you greeted by silence? What even is the alternative? So many of us have never experienced it!

There's a parallel universe somewhere where we started with a clear objective and, over the course of the presentation, we guided our audience using facts, stories, evidence and data to achieve what we wanted. There's a universe where we nailed it. For most of us, it's probably not this universe.

Think back to a recent presentation when you were a member of the audience. Could you articulate the exchange? Its defining purpose? Not the title or content, but the purpose?

The problem with PowerPoint

Over time, we've been tricked by the neat order of templates, 16:9 slides, footers, agendas and a final,

'Thank you.' There's an outward appearance of everything being 'in place' and following an order.

If the deck is neatly formatted, it follows that the ideas must be too, right? The majority aren't. Underneath the formatting, there's just a content dump of slides, a real mess. Take away the slides and the thinking behind it is jumbled. Our reliance on PowerPoint has created two serious problems that lead to failed presentations: a lack of clear objective, and a lack of structure and flow.

There's no clear, understandable objective

Far too often we miss the key central idea – the single belief we want clients to embrace. It gets lost in a sea of content, as we haven't made enough effort or given it enough attention to really make it stand out.

In training, staff communication and complex sales cycles, if we don't start with an objective and keep things clear, even a perfectly designed presentation can't save things. Without a clear objective, there's no North Star to move towards, no way of clearly articulating a benefit to an audience and no way of knowing what's necessary and what's not.

To make an impact, you need to have a clear goal. This isn't just delivering the presentation and moving on. It's understanding what you *want* your audience to *do*. Do you want them to buy something? Collaborate with you? Embrace a new way of thinking? Only then can you know what to aim for.

There's no clear, purposeful structure and flow

Our brains work naturally to organise, categorise and apply meaning to information. We look to make sense of ideas. The linear click/talk, click/talk, slide after slide process is a terribly ineffective way of presenting this. Instead of helping an audience 'get' the journey you're taking them on, they are often overwhelmed by an excess of content without sufficient context or categorisation. Slides can hide huge gaps in logic and processing.

Most presentations don't suffer from a lack of information or slides – there's usually enough of both! There's a tendency to feel we must cover absolutely everything in case we're caught out. We may start off well, but then the anxiety of missing something comes into our heads and there's a tendency to jam in a new slide 'just in case'. Rather than gracefully arriving at our objective at the end of a well-defined route, we blast excessive content at our audience and hope for the best. This shotgun approach overwhelms our audience so much that they stop taking things in – they shut down. The war of attention is lost to too much content.

I'm certain you know the feeling I'm talking about. The presentation you are watching is at slide forty-one but the feeling of overwhelm kicked in at slide twelve and you know you've shut off and you aren't going to remember any of this. 'I'll send you a copy of the deck' is a polite way of acknowledging that this has taken place. The chances are you've also been the cause of it in your own presentations.

Zooming out to make sense

As mentioned, we initially worked a lot in Prezi. Our clients were tired of undifferentiated PowerPoint decks and wanted to try something else, anything else. It was easy to think that the lack of impact was coming from the software and a new alternative would easily solve everything.

Prezi relied on having a big overview screen, or home page, which you would zoom into. This presentation overview was like a map on a large zoomable canvas. As you presented a topic, you would click and zoom in on this map to reveal its content, like going from a map of a country into a state on Google Maps.

With some planning, and done well, it's a cinematic, flowing presentation experience. However, if you skip the planning and place content haphazardly into Prezi, it's a dizzying, nauseating roller coaster of an experience, with your screen spinning out of control. If you've seen a bad Prezi, you'll know exactly what I mean.

The work required to make a great Prezi is organising content in hierarchical order to support this smooth animation.

Before creating a design, we needed to essentially organise and map content in a meaningful way, and ensure things were grouped together in topics. The first step was to decide on a home screen theme, high-level content groups, and then the content in each group.

It would be great if that were the one-click task some clients thought it would be, but it required thinking work and always keeping in mind the goal of the presentation and the journey to get there. This was a far more challenging step than creating artwork or any of Prezi's technical aspects. Before the design work started, we had to map out a storyboard of content. We needed to see how everything fitted together. Clients needed to think deeply about the architecture of their presentation.

This is where the transformation to a much more impactful presentation started to occur; it was the work *before* the Prezi that made their presentation stronger. The Prezi then simply brought it to life in a more visual way. We were experts in assisting clients in this process. And the years of experience seeing the dramatic improvement in the impact clients made led us to develop this clear and practical belief: *Context comes before content.*

We became obsessed about flow and understanding the huge gaps in logic and processing in most presentations. The presentations we created using this approach enjoyed amazing success. Clients had standing ovations, they won deals and they engaged their audiences at workshops and team events. On the surface, it looked to the audience as if Prezi was the main ingredient for this success. In fact, it was the time and effort taken to create the presentation structure that made the biggest difference.

And so, most of our work these days is in PowerPoint. Yep, I said it. We're an award-winning presentation company, experts in the tech we use, and we *choose* to use PowerPoint. Please don't stop reading. Let me explain.

There's no dizziness or nausea if you get it wrong; the price you pay instead is drifting further from your main objective. So, we use the 'context first' mindset and process, and design PowerPoint slides in a different way than most to create Prezi-like decks when clients need them. That's the process I'm going to talk you through.

How to find the end

An entire presentation should be able to be distilled and explained with a high-level 20-30 second overview. That doesn't change, no matter what the presentation is. It's the DNA that sets out the flow of content. If you can't distil your presentation into a high-level overview first, the entire process of creating it is harder and it's not going to make the impact you want it to have.

There are two steps to distilling your presentation: discover and define your objective, and lead your audience towards the objective from the start.

Discover and clearly define your presentation's objective

Before you open PowerPoint, get to your slides, choose images or tinker with your camera positioning to see what your Zoom background will look like, focus in and ask yourself a simple question: 'What is the purpose of this presentation?'

If you can clearly answer this, you are on the path to develop an outstanding presentation. Getting this right has a massively high return on time spent and is easily done, often in less than thirty minutes (but longer if you're working with a group and more discussion is needed).

Even if you're under time pressure to get going creating slides, stop. Do not skip this step. Once you are clear on this question, start to think about what your audience currently thinks and feels. What would you like to change about this? What do they not know that you can help them to solve? Think about this like the process of sharpening an axe: it takes time to get it sharp, but once you're done, it's efficient.

Many people resist this idea as they feel that their presentation is too complex, nuanced or detailed to cut down to one purpose. It's not. We see most presenters trying to communicate three to five objectives on average. It's far more important to communicate what your single big idea is, rather than four that no one will remember.

If you've already adapted to the mindset of a humble servant, it's going to be easier to create your purpose. Make it clear. Very clear. Write it down. Laser focus it.

Once you've got clarity, it's time to write a compelling and attractive headline statement. Think of this presentation title as the first thing you read on a conference agenda or on the screen when you walk into a room. It needs to be impactful and interesting. It's hopefully going to be what the audience remembers and talks about after your presentation. The key here is not to be plain and write just what the content is. Instead, think about newspaper headlines and their role. Aim to create intrigue and package up your content and perspective.

Lead your audience from the start of your presentation to the objective

Imagine reading a book without chapters and with a random placement of pages. Utterly confusing, right? Just adding slides with no sense of order is the same thing. With a clear purpose, the next step is organising your content into clear groups and arranging them in a logical way.

You're looking to map out the journey that will take your audience from the start of your presentation to its clear objective at the end. It gives a framework to what you present. This is the first step in the audience 'getting' what you are speaking about.

Almost all presentations break down into three to five groups of content, and the order you choose for these groups is critical. Taking the time to go through this thinking and processing will make things far easier to follow for your audience.

If you have more than five groups, double-check and consolidate down to five. Don't argue on this one. No, your presentation isn't more complex than every other one I've ever worked on. They all made it work with five groups of content; you can too.

This can take place on a whiteboard or a piece of paper. We've worked out the main title, and now it's time to map your content into groups. If you are stuck or working at the new stages of a presentation, use the titles what, why, who, when & where and how:

- What are you presenting on?

- Why is it relevant or important?

- Who is involved?

- When and where will it take place?

- How?

A strong structure for your content

More advanced and better suited to a narrative presentation is to think of the storyline as a structure. A flow. We will cover this further in Part Three. For more formal presentations like AGMs and Investor Presentations, there is some limit to what you can do as there is a relatively set format. For everything else, it's fair game.

Content can change as you develop the presentation, but you know you've got it right when the structure stays the same. Think about it as a skeleton. A weak spine won't support anything; a strong spine will. This step is one of the many that will also reduce the need for detail-heavy slides.

Now you can fill out the sub-ideas along the page. Jot them down, scribble, cross them out and see if it works. This should be an organic process. It's a chance to check if it makes sense.

Now (and *only* now), open up PowerPoint. You've got your title and divider slides – it's time to write them out as headings. Then add slides as content to these groups and build the slide headings according to the presentation map you've created.

CASE STUDY: 'Do you work with plumbers?'

It was an odd, blunt question to get upfront in a phone call.

'We haven't dealt with too many, but I'm happy to see how we can help,' was my response. That's how the conversation started.

Although the client was originally a plumber, what started as a two-man company had grown over twenty years to a 100-strong, successful, profitable business with a great reputation. The team created engineering solutions and worked on high-rise buildings, airports and complex projects. Based on the success of a previous project, they had now been invited to be a preferred supplier of A-grade commercial development projects to an ASX100 company and the client was booked in to present to the leadership team.

This would be a high-stakes meeting with the potential to transform his business. The only challenge was that this would be his first time giving a presentation.

He'd received some high-level guidance on what the presentation should cover, and the default thinking could easily have been to go into great detail about the business, its capabilities, and the team – you know, the full sales pitch presenting, '100 Reasons We're A Great Option'.

It may have been tempting to feel like 'more is more', but by this stage of the book, you'll know that this is not the right approach...

Following our initial meeting and review of logistics, we spent time focusing on what the presentation's end result should be. Such a broad agenda can be a challenge.

We considered the invitation – which meant the company would already have performed due diligence – but weren't sure exactly who'd be there. What is the approval process in a group that makes such big decisions, and what would they need to make a positive one?

There was a huge gap in the size of the two companies, and while this was probably just another meeting for the ASX100 company, it was going to be the first ever – and most important – formal presentation for our client. It would have been quite easy to get caught in the 'brochure approach' trap, to address the size imbalance or make the mistake of trying to be very formal to match such a big company. Instead, we became laser-focused on developing the purpose.

With the lens of 'The Audience is Number One', we had a few calls made and questions asked. This helped us to understand that our audience were a busy group who were exposed to huge amounts of information and made important decisions all day. They were adept at making quick decisions and were unafraid to probe and ask questions if needed.

From experience, we knew the window of change and opportunity is the period immediately following a presentation; in this case, it would be the time it took to leave the room and walk to the lift. With that in mind, our objective was to influence and frame those few minutes. What would that short, sharp, debriefed conversation sound like? Simply put, we decided it would be, 'Yes, we'll deal with this team.' That was our measure of success. The entire process was about trust and credibility. We came to the conclusion that this was about confidence.

This gave us an insight into how to structure our presentation. The company needed to understand our client's people, capability and commitment to working with them in sharp, purposeful sections. This guided the introduction and the story of how, as an apprentice plumber, the CEO had driven past this company's building sites and had worked hard for over twenty years to be in that room, talking to them as a partner.

A showcase of successful projects followed, then information about the team and how they use software to track project details, and, finally, a look forward at what the company could expect from working with our client: their commitment.

The result? Our client didn't even need to leave the room. It was an on-the-spot confirmation.

Self-assessment and reflection

First download the worksheet and then watch the video example, both available at https://presentationdesign.co/playbook. The next stage is to review a recent presentation you gave or attended, before answering the following questions:

- What was the objective?
- What were the 'groups' of content?

Just to note

By knowing what you want your presentation's end result to be, you'll better understand how to get your audience there. Follow this principle and you'll see that your approach, your content and even your delivery are that much easier to figure out.

6
Power Principle #3: Be Authentically You

If your audience doesn't connect with you, you aren't going to be able to make an impact. There's no better way to connect with people than to be genuine. After so many bad presentations, we're all pretty good at seeing through bullsh!t by now. Don't try to be anybody else. You just need to be you.

'Polished' versus 'authentic'

If I asked you what a high-impact presenter looked like, you might imagine someone larger than life on a conference stage – a high-energy, big venue presentation, with loud music and even a few cheers here and there.

If I then asked about a low-impact presenter, you might picture someone speaking in an energy-sapping monotone, struggling in bad light to read bullet points off a set of slides you feel will never end. You've checked your phone eleven times and would trade anything not to be there. Presentation hell.

We tend to think of the impact of a presentation being tied to its energy level. A high-impact presentation has high energy and low energy creates a low impact. Well, I'm telling you that this isn't true.

In our work behind the scenes with presenters, we get to see them across the full presentation development lifecycle – from their early conversations as clients understanding their goals, working with them on developing their presentation content, refining their deck, and then watching the real-life act of them presenting live on stage or online. We are witnesses to their moments of truth.

Two observations stand out from our experience with these presenters. The first observation is the difference between how clients speak in conversation and how they deliver their presentations. We'd often work with people who'd be great conversationalists, intelligent and engaging in person – but when it came time to put a clicker in their hand and talk to an audience? Injected with a severe dose of presentation anxiety, they'd quickly transform into someone completely different. They'd turn inwards and lose confidence.

As a result, their presentations weren't an accurate reflection of who they actually were as people.

It isn't pleasant to watch someone personable, who can easily win the war for attention in one-to-one settings or small group discussions, struggle to transfer this skill when they present. There is often a huge disparity in how they come across. I'm sure you've seen this happen; maybe it's even happened to you.

The second observation we made was about the path another group of people followed. These were more understated, the softly spoken clients – slightly more introverted, but very smart and still relatable. Quite a few were engineers. In early meetings, I remember thinking that, given the task ahead of them when it came time to present, they'd be toast. But this so often wasn't the case. When it came to deliver, they'd start to deliver their presentation and there was a real transformation. A positive one. They took that conversational, relatable feel from speaking 1:1 and in small groups and were able to apply this to their presentation.

On stage, they looked more comfortable, more genuine and more relaxed. They certainly weren't the most polished, super high-energy presenters, but they did a fantastic job of connecting with their audience.

Something didn't gel for me from these two observations. Some of the highest levels of engagement and success in winning the war and making an impact weren't coming from the most polished presenters. Why did I assume that would be the case? It all came down to my own long-standing biases. Having come from banking, there was a strong link in my mind between the most professional-looking and polished people being the most effective presenters. I'd been in formal settings and seen some fantastic examples of senior bankers in great suits with big titles confidently working the room. But out in the wider world, I wasn't seeing it – that link didn't always exist. It wasn't a reliable predictor.

So, I started to think: was this polished delivery I saw as important *actually* the most important factor? When I thought about it some more, I realised it wasn't. In fact, it's more of a self-defence mechanism. When it comes to being judged, almost all presenters rate 'being perceived as professional' as an important factor. They feel pressured to become a perfectly polished speaker, but it's just not them. They feel as if they're acting out, trying to be someone they're not – all because of the crushing weight they feel standing before a large group.

Time and again, I've seen less polished presenters have a greater impact than more polished ones. This led me to understand that to create a genuine sense of engagement, your audience needs to feel a sense of connection with you. When you're a bundle of nerves reading text from a screen, it's very hard for people to feel anything, as they aren't seeing the real you and can't connect with that. If your sole focus is to be polished, your natural self is hiding away and there's no opportunity for your audience to relate to you as a human.

I'm not saying professionalism isn't important; it is. What I mean is that to make an impact, you need to set your mind to exposing a greater sense of who you are to your audience. Not the flustered, apologetic, excuse-spilling side – no, you're still in a presenter's mindset. *It's about turning up and being authentically you.*

Imagine this. It's your first time formally presenting to an audience. The presentation you're going to give is intensely personal. Oh, and you're doing it live in front of a crowd of 4,000 – plus some expert international presenters – at the Sydney Opera House with thousands more people watching online. Just you. On a stage. For twenty minutes. How would that challenge feel? Does the very idea of it make your heart race and your stomach churn? This is the task Sydney-based martial artist and writer Nadine Champion was given.

CASE STUDY: When your first presentation is a TED Talk

After twenty years of studying under the legendary teacher Benny 'the Jet' Urquidez, Nadine fought and won her biggest battle – against cancer. Friends of hers had witnessed her mental strength and courage throughout her journey, and she was invited to give the closing talk at TEDxSydney 2015.

The challenge was that popping up some slides and presenting aren't a big part of a martial artist's training regime. The Opera House opportunity was going to be her first ever presentation. How do you approach the task of presenting your life story to an audience for the first time?

I'd met Nadine informally and offered to help with her presentation design. This process gave me an insight into the thinking and months of preparation she'd already put into it. Nadine didn't have business presentation experience to draw from. She hadn't developed a presentation persona and didn't have a library of past successful presentations in her head to help her feel she'd be OK. However, her martial arts training had instilled a strong sense of confidence in herself and an ability to be comfortable with discomfort. She'd been tested in many difficult situations and was certain of her ability to remain calm and deliver under pressure.

From the outset, she saw there was no other approach than to be completely authentic. Authenticity starts with bravery and accepting you'll be judged because you know it doesn't have to be the entire audience you're there for; there's just a core group you're looking to speak to directly and connect with. Nadine's advantage was her deep belief and conviction in what she was about to say. Nothing was manufactured; it was stripped back and completely genuine, and she knew that.

On the day, one great speaker followed another – all very experienced and engaging people. As the afternoon came to a close, the lights dimmed and Nadine came out on stage. She started with deeply personal revelations from her life experience, then built up to a moment in her presentation where she put herself under enormous pressure and scrutiny. This could have gone any number of ways but, founded in authenticity, she took a risk. I'm not going to give anything else away; look up Nadine's talk on TEDxSydney's YouTube channel: www.youtube.com/watch?v=r1Zfscuv_YE&t=3s

Nadine received a standing ovation and that same evening she received a call from an agency wanting to capture her story. Today, she travels around Australia and the world as an accomplished professional speaker and has published her story in a fantastic book, *10 Seconds of Courage: How to recognise and embrace those life-changing moments.*

Presenting authentically as yourself will immediately relieve some of the pressure, give you a confidence boost and help generate that magic energy of connection that will allow you to create an impact.

Three steps to being authentically you

When it comes to your moment of truth, aim to follow three simple ideas to immediately transform the task of presenting from something terrifying to – well, not a walk in the park, but at least something manageable, something where you can be a version of yourself. A professional, presenter version, but still a version of you, rather than a bundle of nerves or an over-polished sales pitch.

Be brave

What I mean here is: have the courage – and make the decision – to show the real, authentic version of yourself when you present. Be prepared to be a human, to be fallible, humble and open. Have the confidence to be genuine, have fun, be humorous, take a risk and tell stories that connect emotionally. I don't mean oversharing – don't put absolutely everything out there. Keep things in context. You still need to rehearse and be professional. Just be happy to be you. Being brave changes your relationship with the audience and will connect you on a deeper level than facts and figures ever will.

We also need to acknowledge we don't have to connect with every single attendee and that's OK. We are humans and, for reasons out of your control, not everyone is able to be there with you. They may have had a challenging week or received an urgent work emergency email just before you started talking. It's reasonable that about 10% of your audience may be there physically but not mentally that day; what they're thinking about is more important to them than what you're about to share. That's OK too. It's the core group you're looking to connect with.

Have conviction

You're going to be in front of a group of people saying some things. You'd better believe them, and
if you do, do everything you can to demonstrate
your conviction.

In our modern times, our bullsh!t filters have
improved. We scroll through social media and are
attuned to genuine things. It's easier not to change;
quite a few of us are cynical, fatigued and have a sense
of overload. I don't need to tell you not to lie; that's
obvious and easily done. But don't be lazy and do a
half-job, either – just cruising through on mediocre.

To make an impact, demonstrate an unshakeable conviction in the things you're saying that are important
to your audience. Don't believe that just because you
say it, they'll believe it or accept it. Your audience
needs to feel it. Don't hide that conviction; embrace
it. Look at your content, slides and ideas. Then flip
things around and call bullsh!t on your own content.
If you're offended by it, think about how you can
counter it.

Create that moment of choosing conviction and it will
transform the words you choose, the tone you use to
communicate them, your body language and your
eyes. This rock-solid conviction is incredibly attractive and effective in making you authentic.

Meet the audience where they are

We all lead very different lives, and our mornings, days and inboxes will be unique to each of us. When it comes to a presentation, our runway and our flight path to get there will be different. When you talk to a group, you need to understand the context, the energy and the feeling of the room. Check in, find out and meet people where they are. Then seek to take them on a path.

Anticipate and accept that things could go wrong

When you present, you don't need to be a 10/10. Your audience doesn't expect you to be perfect, so neither should you. In the pressure of presenting, we'd love for things to be perfect, so when bad things happen, they can have a multiplier effect and quickly drain our poise and sense of confidence.

When we've spent hours preparing and something happens that doesn't match what we planned in our heads, it can be terribly off-putting and terminal. Don't allow it. In a live environment, something will go wrong. I guarantee it. Being well prepared is a great counter to this, but will never overcome Murphy's Law. Distractions, technical glitches… expect them; be prepared that they will occur. Look for them. A great counter to perfection is to anticipate these events and then when they happen, note them as the natural way of things happening.

You're also going to slip up and say the wrong thing from time to time. Accept it when it happens, acknowledge it and move forwards. This isn't an excuse for not doing the work or preparation. Don't aim to rely on sympathy instead of delivering. You're there to do a job, so don't make excuses to your audience.

Be yourself and more

If we strip this back, being told to be your authentic self may create a sense of paralysing fear. Relax. It's going to be OK. I appreciate this may sound slightly contradictory because I've just said creating an impact is about being you. We've established that the authentic version of yourself will create a bond and a sense of trust and confidence with your audience.

That's all true in terms of our mindset and how we frame our tasks, focus and preparation. But there's a difference between a conversation and a presentation. In a conversation, there's a two-way ebb and flow. You get the chance to feel the energy of the conversation, and lots of time to stop and listen. But we're talking about presentations here. Everyone stays quiet and gives you attention. When it comes to delivering a presentation, you're looking to command the attention of a group in what's mostly a one-way dialogue.

To do this well and create an impact, you do need to shift your energy higher than its natural state and create an effective presence. This 'presence' doesn't mean you need to run into the room whooping or give the audience high-fives. Of course, you're welcome to try this out on your path to becoming a better presenter and see how you go! What I'd suggest instead for greater effectiveness is a more balanced approach to turning up your inner vibe. You don't need to be someone else when you arrive, but you do need to find an amplified version of yourself in your delivery.

When delivering a presentation, the most successful presenters make an impact by working at a higher level of focus and energy that matches the format they're speaking in. Yes, they're still authentically themselves; it's the same person you'd have a one-on-one conversation with, and they stick to the principles, it's just they're 20% more:

- 20% more energy

- 20% more hand gestures

- 20% louder

- 20% more expressive

With experience, they've worked out who they'd like to be and how they want to come across when presenting. It feels comfortable, and when the time comes, they have a process for switching to this amplified version of themselves.

I hope this sounds reasonable. But you might be wondering how you learn how to make the switch and find an amplified version of yourself that feels comfortable? *You can do this by developing your 'presentation persona'.*

It's not every day that you will get up there to speak, and so this isn't the everyday version of you. It's the presentation version, and by defining this persona's characteristics, you can start to dramatically improve the impact of how you present yourself. It starts as simply as using your time and imagination to reflect on how you'd like to appear to your audience. To help you to do this, consider the answers to some questions:

- What's your aspirational version of your presentation self?

- Who have you seen present, and what are some of the things they've done that you'd like to model?

- What are some of the ways you'd like to define yourself?

- What's the impression you are looking to make?

Take the time to define and write down these characteristics. When it comes time to present, lean into them and bring this persona to life. It may feel like you're faking it, but all you're going to do is find attributes you already have and enhance them a little. You might start by using words like warm, strong and passionate. Not bad as a start. Calm, authoritative and engaging are also great. You're setting out safe, comfortable areas that are authentic and attainable in this aspirational, amplified version of yourself.

The brilliance of being able to shift from the everyday you into a persona is that it gives you permission to try different things you might not ordinarily explore. This could be humour, questions and upping the emotional leverage you're looking to use. Your persona isn't afraid of experimenting. Fear of being judged often creates a feeling of anxiety and vulnerability, alongside a crippling fear of rejection – not a great combination for a presenter. It holds us back, locks us down and stops us from making an impact. Adopting a persona is slightly dissociative and can protect you from some of those feelings. Your confidence comes from accepting it's not you in your entirety that's going to stand up in front of some slides. In your mind, it's your presentation persona being judged, not the entire you. As silly as it might sound, it does help.

When it comes to 'being' more, 20% more energy, gestures, volume, expression, etc, is a reliable guideline, but there may be times you need to adjust that 20% to meet your audience. If you're presenting at a large venue with a stage, you're going to need to take it up a bit extra, maybe 30% or even 40% more. On the other hand, a boardroom style, seated conversational presentation needs to be pared back, but still needs an effective means of asking open questions.

Your 20% may not be sustained throughout the course of your delivery, either. We'll explore the concept of modulation and its benefits later in the book. For now, it's safe to say it's not always just 20% more everything. It could at times be 20% less too, or 20% more intense, but otherwise normal.

When you're presenting online, the persona development step is essential because the preparation steps leading up to delivery are removed. We also lose a lot of the external prompts that help us mentally prepare and step into the role of a presenter.

In a face-to-face environment, these subconsciously help us prepare and make the switch. Online, we may be contending with building works next door or energetic dogs and kids in the background – everyday things that pull us away from the mindset we need to make the switch and be effective.

Gauging your online presentation audience is particularly challenging and can lead to some mismatches. A small green light doesn't tell you if you're doing well or not, nor does it provide you with any energy to feed off like a live audience might.

I've found most online presentations fall slightly short as it's challenging to sustain a higher state of energy when presenting online. So, consider that your online persona may need to be even higher energy than your face-to-face one.

Find yourself. Be brave. Let your audience feel your authenticity. Sometimes, you need just ten seconds to find it.

Self-assessment and reflection

This chapter is about being authentically you, but what does that mean? Take a few minutes to consider the traits you have that motivate you. Do you show them when you present, or could you be more?

This is the start of building your presentation persona. Describe it in a sentence. What are the three words you can use to sum it up?

Now watch Nadine's video if you haven't already. What do you think you can do to find your ten seconds?

Just to note

Embrace authenticity. Define your persona; be comfortable with what it is. Own it. When it's time to present, by making that switch to another planned version of you, you're already on your way to making an amazing impact.

7
Power Principle #4: Assume Apathy

Your audience needs to be as interested in what you present as you are. It's your job to make them. That's the challenge you're up against.

Make your ideas interesting

In most presentations, failure isn't as dramatic as a ceiling falling down, a room full of heckling and boos or the audience walking out in protest. A presentation's main failure is usually more subtle. Your idea goes nowhere, connections aren't made or problems remain unsolved even after the audience has heard your solution. It's silent, passive resistance to what you present and an unmoved audience.

If you're considering your audience's needs, being their humble servant, beginning with the end in mind, following a structure and being authentically you, then you've already built a strong foundation for breaking through this resistance and making an impact.

Here's another principle that will greatly assist. Start with the assumption no one really cares about what you're planning to present, and that your job is to make them care. When you work with a certain subject matter every day, you can quickly lose objectivity when communicating. This presents two clear barriers when presenting:

1. You can easily assume everyone has at least an equal understanding of your subject matter.

2. Your day-to-day familiarity with your subject matter might mean you're missing the wonder of it, that is, the magic it takes to bring the audience into your world.

Find your magic offering

The starting point in embracing this principle is to ask yourself what the difference is between your presentation taking place and not taking place. Unless you're revealing how to survive a shark attack or have cracked the code to cure illnesses, it's unlikely the audience will be on the edge of their seats or glued to the screen waiting with bated breath.

Be honest and ask yourself: what happens if I fail to appear? What happens if the internet cuts out completely, and my Zoom presentation doesn't happen? Ask yourself this question from the audience's perspective. Will your failure to reach the audience have a dramatic impact on their lives? Take your time here. Think with your head and examine with your heart. Dig deep and find those reasons. If you've spent time on this and still can't, then throw everything out the window, reset and find a new lens.

Assuming apathy is a healthy dose of self-imposed realism that forces you to focus on creating value and a fair exchange with your audience. Once you've adopted this principle and are clear on the fact that what's important to you may not be as important to everyone else, you're in a good place.

It should now be clear that your task as a presenter is to move people from where they are to a future state. That's not going to happen by luck or good fortune; it's up to you and you should feel energised to do it. We'll cover some of the more tactical ways to do this later in the book, but what we're looking to do here is set out a guiding principle.

We've already established that most presentations are time-fillers that will never make a difference or impact. To be a better presenter, you need to appreciate this and use your focus to make sure what you do has some sort of meaning. If you don't care, or don't appreciate this, the change you want won't happen. The wall of passive resistance will win. Your job is to be a persuasive presenter. It's not up to your audience to pretend to care. It's up to you to persuade them. You don't need a hammer; you need a velvet glove.

Think about the Greeks

Long before corporate presentations, Aristotle and the Greeks relied on the effectiveness of their communication. Without a slide deck and a clicker in the Greek court, ideas and people would live and die based on how persuasively they presented their arguments – a true case of naked presenting. Their approach to governance and organisation remains a key foundation for how we govern today.

In any presentation you want some change from our audience. To achieve this, you need to be persuasive. So, how did the Greeks approach it? They believed in the power of rhetoric to persuade and inform. That is, to be effective and have others accept your argument (so you advance on the path to change something), your argument (presentation) must use a mix of ethos (credibility), logos (reason) and pathos (emotion). Aristotle believed an imbalance in these tools – or omitting one – would significantly reduce the power of rhetoric.

In the corporate presentation, this approach can either be used as deep inspiration or a simple checklist. Too often, we see the real-world failures or let-downs when these factors aren't present. There may be elements of each, or they may all be there, but the balance may be out or they aren't as strong as they should be.

Ethos

Ethos is the Greek term for character and in an argument, it's about establishing credibility. Your audience is far more likely to engage with your attempt to persuade them when they feel you're experienced, well established or an expert in what you do. While we're familiar with this in our own mind, it's an important element in your presentation that needs careful balance. If you undersell yourself, your audience may miss some of your wonderful and unique characteristics.

At the same time, we hold a particular disdain for presenters who push ethos too far: too much and it's considered bragging. I'd also be careful about external references that can come across as name-dropping. It's a fine line.

Whether the audience is processing your message systematically or heuristically, your ability to convey authority (or expertise) is fundamental. People's willingness to take what you're saying at face value is directly proportionate to how credible they feel you are. Your audience will be asking themselves a simple question: does this person know what they're talking about? Make sure you give them a reason to answer yes.

If you're completely uncomfortable with a strong personal ethos, think about addressing it in the case studies and examples you use as an external endorsement:

- Who have you worked with?

- What has your success been?

- What have other people said about you?

- What awards and recognition have you earned?

Authority can be conveyed in a number of ways, and very much depends on your audience. A scientist may wish to use their academic credentials, but in business, those mightn't be effective. A business leader looking to persuade an audience might refer to their previous roles in similar companies or list their achievements. The form this takes is very much industry-specific, but it's extremely important you communicate your authority to your audience before you attempt to convey your message.

CASE STUDY: Underdoing ethos

Ethos was an important component to address with a client who'd been invited to an international conference to showcase a product she had developed as a natural approach to men's contraception.

Feeling the pressure of speaking at such a high-profile event, she asked us to assist in the developing and design of her presentation. Having a medical background, she had a natural tendency of establishing credibility via papers and qualifications, but she was extremely shy about pushing too hard on her personal ethos. This wasn't a purely medical conference though – there was a wider audience from the business, government and medical sectors.

Looking at the client's original presentation draft, the first few pages were full of facts and information. When we started to drill down with some questions about her background and approach, it emerged that only she and one other person had the knowledge and technical research capability to develop the product. They were international experts and after years of hard work were close to a major scientific breakthrough that could change the world.

This fact was relevant because it would influence the audience's openness to accepting her argument. They wouldn't have known it otherwise, so it needed to be prominent in her presentation positioning as it supported the rest of what she was going to share.

Some people feel that this element pushes them towards selling themselves and they shrink from that. Don't sell yourself short. It makes a huge difference.

Logos

Google exists, and your presentation isn't a brochure. These are already self-service forms of information your audience can access without having to listen to you waffle on. Repeating well-known facts or quotes is a waste of your time and theirs.

Logos is an appeal to logic. In a presentation, it's your role to expertly guide the audience through the building blocks of an argument and show them that the outcome just makes sense. Far too often, we just talk about how we see the world and what an idea is. It's a blunt, 'Agree with me or disagree with me.' You're far more likely to have an audience accept an idea, fact or figure when they themselves can break down an idea and where it came from so they can follow the logic and hopefully come to the same conclusion.

Simon Sinek's often quoted *Start with Why* TEDx Talk is a beautiful example of logos in action. He states the outcome of his thinking upfront. If that was where he left it, it's just another opinion. But by stepping you through how that thinking works, you understand what's behind it; it then becomes something you're more likely to embrace. Clients mention that clip frequently, and I think it's not just the idea; it's the skilled art of logos that also resonates so strongly with them.

When you present assumptions, outcomes or ideas that needed a thinking process, don't assume your audience will agree. Share that process, facts and resources so that they can come to a similar conclusion.

Pathos

Pathos is an appeal to your audience's emotional side – presenting something in a way that makes them feel differently – and that emotion in turn helps them embrace an idea or change their mind.

One of the most common goals clients have is to create a more story-based approach to their presentations. Stories are the wrapping we put around ideas, experiences and insights that add emotion to them. We most commonly and easily reject new ideas and requests because they don't appeal to or change our emotional state. We're not good at appealing to emotions when we present.

The skilled approach to pathos isn't pleading, guilt or weakness. How often do you listen to and engage with people who use tactics like that? Instead, it's connection, authenticity and vulnerability. It's an appeal to the heart, the stoking of desire or increasing fear – helping your audience *feel*.

An argument or presentation with pathos may touch our hearts, but what it's really doing is activating a different area of our brain. When a connection with our emotions is made, it creates an emotional saliency that creates a stronger feeling and increases the brain's priority in remembering it. If you're in a senior position, people have to do what you tell them. Pathos is the iron fist in a velvet glove that changes their mind and helps them feel they *want to*, rather than *have to*.

This approach is about stopping the linear path of information and introducing personal experiences. It needs to be authentic, as we've discussed. When introducing a new idea, observation or goal, share a personal insight about where it came from. These things don't come out of nowhere. Share the origin of a business, team or product. Share change with a personal insight as to how it will affect people. If you're trying to change something, acknowledge upfront how that looks in day-to-day experience – both good and bad.

Understand how you came to think a certain way – how values were formed and the story of why things are important to you. Stop and ask questions of yourself and the audience. Give a contrasting view of the future: *if this happens, here's what it will look like...*

It's about understanding that we are humans and being one yourself when you present. The good news is that it's not hard to do. That means it's one of the areas you can improve and see immediate results in during the dreary 3:00pm session.

CASE STUDY: Making a team feel it

Working with fantastic clients has given us the opportunity to see how powerful an impact presenters can have when their focus is on making the audience feel something. Several years ago, we were engaged to design a retrospective presentation on a government medical team's three-year result for their internal conference.

One of the presentations was to open the conference: the leadership team were looking to show staff and stakeholders the initiatives they had launched as a team and a scorecard on the impact they were having on organisational goals.

It was a high-stakes presentation full of facts, figures and survey results. In theory, it ticked all the boxes, but it didn't feel quite right. It wasn't balanced. There was very little pathos.

Behind the facts, these health professionals cared deeply about their community, their role, and delivering quality services to those who needed them. They had a strong purpose and their dedication to this was obvious when we talked with them, but none of it was present in their presentation.

As we went through their existing PowerPoint, stuck at the end of the slides, after all those numbers and details, were a few small client quotes as proof points of the impact they had with their clients. They had been put in there almost as an afterthought. There was a proof in those words that bought to life the qualitative impact the team had made on people they cared deeply about. This was our pathos.

With sufficient time and budget, we may have been able to film some case studies, but we had neither – and it was tricky to put people on camera. These were the hidden stories that weren't being shared, yet happened daily at the frontline and were making a genuine difference. We suggested that the team revisit some of their clients at home and, with their permission, record short thirty-second audio clips of them speaking about their experiences. These clips were easy to embed in the presentation from a technical standpoint – at the end of each of the presentation's four sections, we had a minimalist screen, simply showing redacted client details. Being able to hear their voices – genuine, authentic people speaking – was the focus. It wasn't polished, but it was real. It bought their mission to life.

The result? There were tears among some of the team that day. They felt it. It unified them and reaffirmed their deep commitment to their clients, each other and their shared purpose.

If you're looking to move people to change, connect with how they feel.

Self-assessment and reflection

Identify the ethos of your presentation. Make sure you've established it so it's clear to your audience.

With a recent presentation, review and respond to the following questions:

- Where was your credibility?

- Which logos elements were present?

- Which ethos elements were present?

Just to note

No one will care what you have to say unless you make them. That's what you have to assume to begin with. Then you can build up a blend of credibility, logic and emotion that makes them care. Get that right and you'll feel the impact just like your audience will.

8
Power Principle #5: Prepare To Overdeliver

When your moment of truth arrives, don't make a half-hearted effort and hope for the best. Set yourself up for success by considering the before, during and after of your presentation.

Preparation is key

When you're pushed for time, preparation is going to be the part you'll feel most tempted to skip and the part of your presentation that will suffer. Often it feels like enough of an achievement to get the deck done on time and then turn up to deliver so you've already ticked the box.

Preparation is the sacrifice you think you can make that doesn't cost you. That is, until you start the presentation, the nerves kick in, things start feeling lost, and the only thing you want to do is wrap things up and pretend this the nightmare didn't happen. How's this for a first impression?

'Is this mic working?'
'Can everyone hear me?'
'Hang on; why's it doing this?'
'Can you see my screen?'
'Won't be a minute folks.' *Awkward silence*

It's incredibly difficult to make an impact when the opening of your presentation reveals you decided to wing it on the day and now the audience is watching you do the things you should already have taken care of. It's a misstep, hard to come back from, and isn't part of a fair exchange between you and the audience.

It doesn't have to be this way. Preparation is one of the few elements entirely in your control. Every extra minute you prepare has an enormous return on time spent. Common amongst all impactful presenters isn't the model of remote clicker they use, their opening sentence or their favourite font. Instead, they all share a dedication to being overprepared:

- They know their audience better. They've prepared by researching their audience.

- Their content seems ripe, mature and thought out – they've thought about what they need to say and the most engaging way to communicate facts, stories and ideas.

- They have a smooth flow of delivery – they've practised and prepared their delivery in their head and out loud so that they know what their specific impactful moments are.

- They have fewer technical issues and know how to use their equipment – their presentations are smooth events that flow even if there are delivery or technology hiccups.

When you add up all these points, the result is presenters who are more confident and clearer, and enjoy a greater level of engagement with their audience. Make the commitment to be the one who doesn't just tick the box for the bare minimum of preparation; instead, wholeheartedly overprepare.

Begin with a checklist

When time starts to run down and the nerves kick in, it's easy to lose composure and not know where to focus our attention. Things start to scatter and it's easy to spend time jumping around making minor formatting changes to our slides or going over things we already know.

Rather than wait for that moment, create a detailed checklist that covers the four key components of your presentation (I'll tell you what these are, don't worry) and try to write three to five action items for each.

It's easy: four different areas with three to five things in each. Now instead of jumping around, you have a clear plan to tackle your remaining tasks. It's the start of the process of being a presenter that systematically overprepares and enjoys greater success. Each presentation has its own unique variables, so your list will look different to everyone else's, but the four areas will remain the same:

1. **Content and audience**. Gaining clarity on who you are presenting to, and how to present as a humble servant, will create a fair exchange:

   - What's relevant?

   - What's the agenda for the day?

   - What does the day look like to them – before and after?

   - Which recent events are front of mind?

   - How do they connect to what you're presenting?

2. **Your deck.** Ensuring you have a balanced, well prepared, checked presentation:

   - Well-formatted deck with embedded fonts.

   - The correct aspect ratio.

- Embedded videos and tested animations.

- Have a backup of your presentation available on another device or medium.

3. **Rehearsal.** Ask yourself a set of questions about the layout and overall run through of the environment:

   - How big is the audience, and what does the room look like?

   - Will it be boardroom style, theatre style, etc? (We ask this question to optimise presentation design, and I've always been surprised at how little thought is given to this.)

   - What is the format and layout of the area speakers use to set up?

4. **Technology.** Technology will fail. We know this, but it's about reducing any impact:

   - Ensure you have a battery pack, chargers, cords and attachments.

   - Install the latest software updates on the device you'll be using.

   - Close any extra applications you won't be using.

   - Turn on a 'Do not disturb' function.

   - Have a backup of your presentation available on a USB key / flash drive.

Once you start creating your list, you'll probably include a lot more than the three to five items for each. The bigger the checklist the better; it's a sign of your commitment to overpreparing. A dedication to overpreparing means practice. This, in turn, creates a more natural balance between you as the presenter and your visual aid: the deck.

During the height of the COVID pandemic, we saw a great deal of presenters who'd worked face-to-face struggle to make the change to online interaction, mostly by making a series of technical errors that were largely avoidable. Don't be one of them. Take your preparation seriously and you're already a better presenter.

CASE STUDY: The cost of not preparing

Several years ago, a large multinational company's local team engaged us to assist in the creation of a high-stakes pitch of a safety and audit training package to the federal government.

They were a great team of smart, accomplished professionals who were looking to wow their clients with an amazing Prezi. They'd become so used to presenting in a formal environment that they could pitch off the top of their heads at a moment's notice. In fact, using Prezi meant that they themselves weren't feeling tested enough, and were a bit bored of doing things the same way.

Time was tight. We only had a forty-eight-hour window to deep dive and familiarise ourselves with the presentation's structure, content and flow so the team could undertake the process of designing it. Short, tight turnarounds increase risk; the adrenalin was high in those last few hours and the team needed to focus, but we got it done.

On the day, the team were full of confidence in their fantastic new presentation and had pitched so many times they felt preparation was unnecessary. They had the experience and flexibility to work out whatever presented itself.

It didn't start well. As the team's first presenter loaded up the presentation, hopes were high. The introductions were done and then the first click was made to kick off the presentation. Nothing happened. Click. Nothing. Disaster was unfolding.

It took over five minutes to work out the technology, and the impact was disastrous. There were apologies. However, in that moment of truth, it didn't make sense to the client that a team specialising in safety and audit training should make such a rookie mistake.

Needless to say, they weren't invited to the next round and the client's formal feedback read, 'We welcome new ideas and approaches but if you are trying something new, we trust that you take the time to test and become proficient in it before taking it to us.'

Ouch. Being overconfident and failing to prepare cost them millions of dollars in potential revenue. Not all failures will be so disastrous, but they all will be an enormous barrier to making an impact.

Make the commitment to be a part of the small group of presenters that overprepare. Break this down into a checklist and give yourself a solid foundation to do your best and enjoy the success it creates.

Keep your audience fully engaged

One of the major challenges we have in making an impact in presenting is simply keeping an audience engaged throughout – to win and maintain their attention. How often do you find that a presentation ends up feeling like a lecture? You watch the clock wind down just waiting to get out of there.

Understanding the flow of energy of your presentation and deliberately engineering how your audience will feel along the way is a preparation tool that anyone can use.

If you think about the engagement in a forty-five-minute corporate presentation, with X being time and Y being engagement, the general experience is this: we start off, cover a lot of information, and start to get bogged down. Then, towards the end, we start to pick up speed as the end is in sight. Too much talking and too little interaction makes it all feel like hard work and an audience turns off. Most often it looks like this:

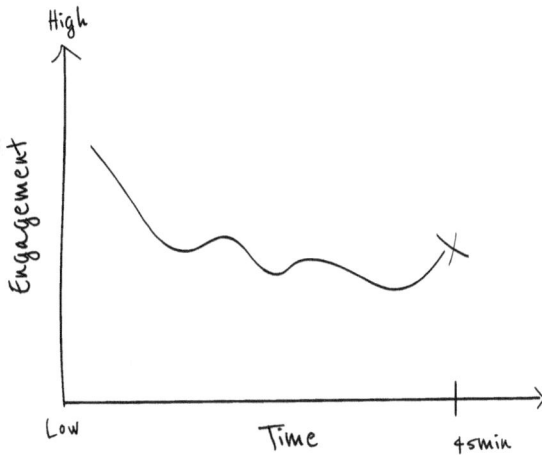

If you can reflect on your last presentation, grab a pen and paper and see if you can map the engagement journey. How did it go?

If you want to make an impact, start to map out where the ups and downs are across the time allocated. Think about your audience's emotional energy and plan targeted strategies to create shifts in it. You don't need to reinvent your presentation so you run at high speed the whole time. That's exhausting. Instead, to achieve impact, you need to plan to purposefully modulate your connection. Different presentations roll out in different ways; some build slowly, and others are more frenetic. It's not just about the start and finish, it's the shifts that happen that sustain attention throughout.

Think about a comedian during a one-hour set. There's a whole stage, with just them and a microphone. They work hard at modulation, variety and surprise.

Great presenters often have a natural or innate ability to understand this; they naturally build high and low points into their delivery. They create an interesting journey. The next time you present, here's a plan for doing this:

Step 1: Draw a chart

We know what the average presentation looks like from the example above, but if you take the time to build and reveal, it could look like this:

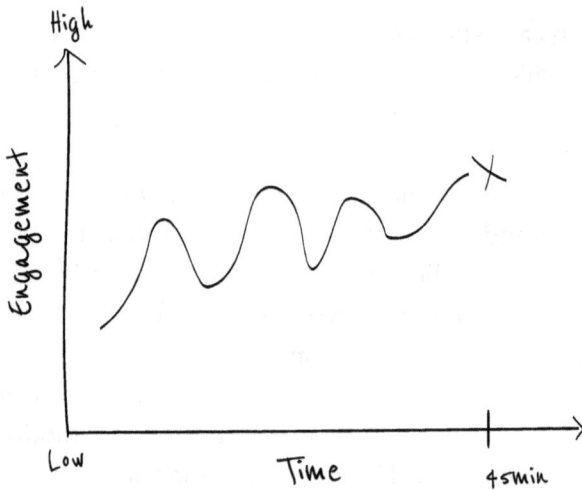

Be conscious of design and start to reflect on moments in your presentation that will drive change. Are they short and sharp like this?

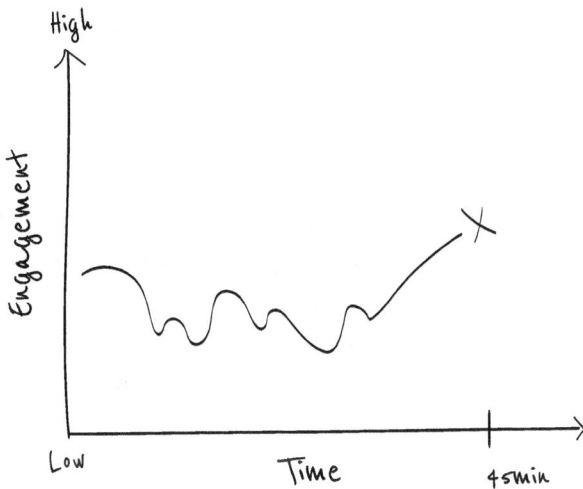

Or is it more of a narrative that will slowly build, increasing tension through each part, and finally come to a great crescendo of engagement?

If it's technical or data-heavy, how about this?

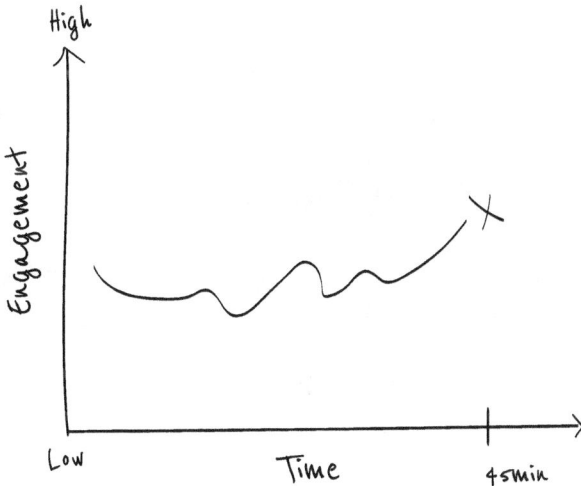

As a trainer or workshop facilitator, you're likely to be thinking actively about your modulation, but what does it look like on a chart?

Firstly, start strong to create an impact, then map how each section will help you to hold back or push forward along the way. You might plan a burst of energy at the start of each section or after your audience has had a moment to consider something – a question, provocative statement or reflection perhaps.

When you're looking to change the way people think, be influenced by your opinion, or come to a set course of action, it's helpful to build along the way. That is, each chapter or section of the presentation comes in strong within the next and, ultimately, ends higher than when you started.

Step 2: Work out your strategies

If you've mapped out your groups and content, now you can look across your chart and examine your strategies and tactics to shift energy. The two things that you are looking to overcome are:

1. You talking and your slides being the main focus. The solution to this is variety:

   - Move to a different part of the room.

   - Build purposeful pauses into the process.

   - Turn off the slides and tell a story.

- Say something shocking.

- Play a video.

- Ask someone else to present part of your content.

- Use props or secondary visual aids such as a flipchart.

2. A lack of interaction and engagement. The elements you can use to shift these are:

- Ask a question.

- Start a discussion.

- Use a case study.

- Run a poll.

- Set an activity.

Step 3: Look out for surprise moments

When we try to recall presentations, we often start with key moments, snippets, images, facts or details. The reason we recall them isn't just that they were interesting; we had an emotional connection with them. If your presentation contains any of these elements you want people to remember, you need to recognise these and build emotional responses around them:

- You could do this by keeping things at a low energy and then providing a strong contrast.

- You could use a long pause followed by a reveal.

- You could talk through an idea, and then reveal something in complete contrast to it.

You can repeat these techniques at various points throughout your presentation. Craft the high-impact moments, so they have the intended effect.

CASE STUDY: The best ever

It's early evening and I'm standing in the lobby of a plush, inner-city hotel at an industry event, surrounded by fifty to sixty speaking professionals, deep in conversation, enjoying each other's company and an evening drink. The conversation stops when a warm, booming, commanding voice comes from one side of the hall.

'Ladies and gentlemen, if you'd kindly follow me.'

Two large doors to a conference room open, and I can hear jazz playing. As we make our way to the entrance, we're welcomed by an open-armed, well-dressed, smiling gentleman.

'Thank you. Please find your seat. This way...' We shake hands. Inside the room, dozens of bright red balloons cover the floor. A stunning image of the theatre is on the screen. At the front of the room is an energetic, dashing gentleman in a smart-cut Savile Row suit, with a smile that warms the room. He spots a friend close by, makes eye contact with her, then takes her hand and they start cutting up the stage with graceful dance steps in perfect unison.

It's the start of a presentation, but like nothing I've ever seen.

I move to my seat and notice each one has a bright yellow rubber duck on it. I don't know why, but I'm intrigued.

I've entered the world of Peter Merrett, a professional speaker, purveyor of wonder, and one of the best examples of someone completely dedicated to his audience. Peter doesn't just turn up; he takes over. Not with an over-the-top, loud personality, but with style meeting substance. It's a wonderful experience.

Over the next forty minutes, Peter guides us through five stories of businesses that have created a sense of wonder in the way they work with their customers. He delivers humour, compassion and business insights flawlessly. He initiates engagement with the audience and then maintains it the entire time. He gracefully ends with a release of roses, and a call to action for us all to think of the moments of wonder we can create for our own customers.

Wow.

In an audience full of experienced presenters, Peter has engineered a session that has resonated deeply with them. They're moved. They feel it. And it isn't a one-off. He's done this dozens of times locally and internationally, bringing conferences of thousands of people in the US to a standing ovation.

With so much complexity to his work, so much can go wrong. How does he manage to consistently engineer high-impact, standout presentations to so many groups? *The difference is his mindset.*

Peter's first career was in five-star luxury hospitality in the UK. He had years of rigorous training on the importance of anticipating and exceeding guests' expectations. With a complete focus on what people think and feel – and using careful planning and preparation – an event can become an experience. It's a mindset and skillset he has transferred to the world of paid, professional speaking and made a success.

He has a clear vision of what he wants for his audience. He has an innate ability to understand the chart. Then, breaking his process down into a checklist and a methodical process means he has confidence in his ability to pull off reasonably complicated logistics. So, when he's presenting, he can be in the moment, be human, connect, make an impact, and move us. You can check out Peter's work and his house of wonder here: https://petermerrett.com

I hope it's not a surprise when I tell you that this book isn't going to transform you into a master presenter like him. But even so, maybe you'll be able to find an opportunity to add a little moment of wonder for your audience if you follow these tips. I encourage you to take just a moment to consider a plan, then keep it in mind as you rehearse and deliver.

This will be something that starts to change the way you present. If you don't have a presentation coming up soon, start doing this when you watch others, and look at what you can incorporate on that basis. This is a simple principle that provides a high return on the time you spend practising it.

Self-assessment and reflection

What three things do you find you struggle with in your preparation?

With the 5 Power Principles in mind, what do you need to focus on to prepare in terms of:

- Content and audience?
- Design and logistics?
- Rehearsal?
- Delivery?

You can download our checklist at https://presentationdesign.co/playbook.

Just to note

You can spot an unprepared presenter in the first second after a new slide. They look at it, read it and remind themselves what they've got to say. A prepared presenter knows what's coming up before they click – they're 'ahead of the deck' and are the more comfortable for it. They introduce ideas and then have the slide reinforce or challenge them.

Which one do you want to be?

PART THREE
THE 4D PROCESS

I've already given you the 5 Power Principles and you're going to find that these will guide you in not just how to present, but how to think about presenting.

But there are still areas to improve. You need to actually be able to create a presentation as well! That's what this section will cover: generating an idea and building the content and slide deck from there, before nailing the delivery.

9
Our Proven Professional Presentation Process

Wow, what a mouthful. But trust me, it's worth learning about. This is the actual process we use at Presentation Design Co. That doesn't mean it's some complex, high-level strategy that only professionals can understand. We try to make our lives easy too, after all. But we know, and have proven time and again, that this simple process delivers results. And that's what I want for you too.

It's a simple, step-by-step process

In our daily work with clients, a project brief often begins with a client emailing a deck accompanied by messages like, 'Any chance you can do something with this?' or, 'Can you shoosh it up a bit?' or, 'We are sick of looking at this deck and have to present on Friday. Please help!'

So, where do we start? Is it about getting the branding right? What font size should it be? Have we got the logo on each page? Can we take some slides from the last deck? Do I need to replace the images?

Firstly, chill out. When it comes to starting work on creating your presentation, there are often so many things that will come to mind. It can be overwhelming, confusing and easy to become lost, waste time and have your anxiety blow up.

The answer is to break it down to a process and a series of steps. What I'd like to share with you is the 4D Process that we use to take clients from that initial first step all the way through to the end. It's a process that we've used to consistently create amazing results for over ten years.

Knowing what the steps are and the sequence they should be in will give you clarity. Once you've started thinking about creating your presentation as a step-by-step production process, we can start identifying specific challenges and barriers and devise actions to overcome them.

These improvements can be small, easy to implement and offer quick wins that have a high return for the overall project – all very useful when operating under time limitations and high expectations.

What is the 4D Process?

If you're looking to make an impact with your presentation, you should be aware by now that you first need to develop a goal and create a benchmark within each step.

1. **Define** the structure

    The goal: To have a clear intent, a well-organised structure and engaging, widely understood content.

    Do this by: Developing the architecture of your presentation, organising key content and developing a well thought out flow from the beginning to end of the presentation.

2. **Develop** dynamic content

    The goal: To bring to life your key ideas in a way that is compelling and clearly understood.

    Do this by: Creating and collating content, ideas, insights and data around each key group within your presentation structure.

3. **Design** distinctive visuals

    The goal: To create a professional visual aid that looks great and supports your presentation.

    Do this by: Designing your slide deck to a professional Tier 1 standard.

4. **Deliver** with distinction

The goal: Feel confident and prepared so that your delivery is effective and engaging.

Do this by: Practising focus, developing a constructive mindset and being prepared.

A balanced presentation is equally strong across all four steps and will deliver an effective and powerful result. While working through these steps, you'll likely discover that you already possess a natural strength in one or more of these areas. That's great! But there is a risk involved too. Experience tells us that the more ability a presenter has in one category, the more likely they are to overlook the others. As much as possible, you'll want to place equal energy on all four steps to achieve the best outcome.

As a team with ten years of experience working with hundreds of great clients, we've viewed many of these ideas and also successfully developed our own. We offer specific concepts across all four steps that we suggest that you pick up, test, advance and develop to further improve the presentation process to suit your own arena, style and topic. The right path will emerge when these tactics are linked together.

Check-in time

How would you rate yourself in terms of your current ability in each of these, and your potential?

1. **Define:** Current __ / 10   Potential __ / 10
2. **Develop:** Current __ / 10   Potential __ / 10
3. **Design:** Current __ / 10   Potential __ / 10
4. **Deliver:** Current __ / 10   Potential __ / 10

Just to note

The 4D Process gives you a way to begin with clear intent and create engaging content. There's no need for me to waffle on here – let's dive straight into the first D.

10
Define The Structure

If time were limited and I had just one piece of advice to give from all my experience of working on presentations, it wouldn't be a secret power word that enthrals an audience, or a PowerPoint hack that will save you hours or a stunning statistic. It's that a structure is the essential ingredient for organising how you communicate.

Chunk your content into groups

This is the magical secret to improving the process of creating an impactful presentation. Organising your thoughts into a meaningful structure and flow transforms how you lay out your presentation.

We use the same process for reports, books and essays, so why not our presentations? The truth is that the linear nature of slide after slide in PowerPoint has allowed our brains to become lazy. It's taken that process of considering our groups and our flow away from us, so now our default practice in a presentation is simply to treat our topics, data and points of knowledge on a slide by slide basis.

When we then present, the audience sees the slides sitting in a flat, evenly spaced, linear format, which suggests that the content has been purposefully thought out. But we know it hasn't been, and the audience will quickly realise that too. A generic approach like this can mask poorly gathered content, when the real goal is to connect and flow information in an efficient way. It also feeds into the idea that the more slides there are, the more persuasive or effective the presentation will be. It's a like writing a book, then swapping around and adding pages and expecting it to still make sense. It won't!

The good news is that this critical first step of a presentation is a very straightforward and simple one that anyone can do. And by anyone, I'm talking to you. You can do this with whatever presentation you've got to make way better quickly and easily. I mean 20% better, maybe even 50%. Huge.

Trust me on this, and you'll see what I mean when you try it for yourself. By focusing first on your structure and creating the flow of your presentation, you'll unlock a new sense of clarity, a sense of ease, you'll know where your content should go, and you'll find yourself able to generate content and ideas that make a much bigger impact.

Four main structures you can use

We've established that effective presentations group content in a meaningful way. The details in each group serves to illustrate, educate, and inform the journey. But what does a meaningful structure actually look like? As the architect, your task is to direct the viewer's attention, and guide them from an engaging start to a destination where a conclusion or decision can be made. You are planning how to guide your audience to what you want them to think, feel, know, and take action on.

In Power Principle #2 (Start with the end in mind) we explored the process of mapping out your presentation into groups and gave you a worksheet to do this. That's the starting point of your structure: looking at three to five groups of content. Now it's about going deeper into this and examining the most compelling ways to arrange those groups according to the type of presentation. There are hundreds of potential options, but I believe these four will work for over 80% of business presentations:

1. Explanation – The Ws

If your task is to explain a concept, idea or a product to your audience, this is the easiest and most practical of the structures. Establish the who, what, when, where and how of what you are presenting and choose the order that you present these in. The Ws are the fundamental way of organising your presentation into an order that most makes sense and is effective.

This structure is going to force you to put your content in an order that makes sense to your audience. The route you take to cover each W is largely down to intuition. As long as you remember that your goal is to make the subject easy to understand, you can't go too far wrong. Let's break the formula down even further with an example of how to approach it.

EXAMPLE: Pitching a new strategy

Imagine you are a manager presenting to your team about a new strategy you want to launch.

- What? Define the challenge in the business that this strategy will solve.

- Why? Explain the context: the impact that this challenge would have if it wasn't addressed and the opportunity that will come from what you are suggesting.

- Who and where? Outline how wide the challenge and solution extend, who the stakeholders are and the roles they need to play.

- How? The details of how this change will happen, what's involved and what you need from the team you're presenting to.

What you end up with addresses all the aspects of your strategy in a very clear and understandable way. You've considered your audience and rather than slide after slide of information, you're packaging your content into digestible groups. This will naturally encourage the curiosity and processing that you need from your audience in order for you to have an impact.

2. Sales – The Three Rooms

Would you like to sit through a forty-minute sales presentation showcasing just how great the presenter thinks they and their business or service are? Like hell! Most sales presentations fail because they aren't persuasive enough, if at all. It's often a case of the presenter thinking that their path to success is to assemble enough content as evidence of how great something is and then expect a yes. That's the pitch: throw it out there and hope for the best.

Instead, we can set the goal to shift from throwing content at an audience to carefully guiding their thinking and feeling to what we want from them. That's a shift from being a pitch to a strategic narrative. We are sharing with them a different view of the world and asking them to consider it as we take them on a journey.

To move from just pitching to presenting, we use something we call the Three Rooms structure. The concept is that you take your audience through three stages (or rooms) before they arrive at the final conclusion (hopefully, saying yes to your pitch). These stages cover context, outcome and proof. I like to imagine them as three rooms of a factory with a production line running through. The first room pulls together the basic shape from the raw materials, the second adds the features and the third finishes it off with a nice glossy coat of paint and a neat box. That really illustrates how you need all three stages, in the right order, to get the outcome you want.

This is a strategical narrative device you can use in PowerPoint to communicate the features and benefits and provides a clear, effective structure in how to build a path through your presentation.

Room 1. Rather than starting with an 'About Us' slide, your first section of content frames the context or your view of the world that your audience can align to. You can do this by articulating:

- A change or shift in the world that's taking place

- The impact that this is having

- How there will be winners and losers from this change

Do this well and you've created something interesting and engaging; you are starting to tell a story. If this view of the world doesn't align with your audience, that's OK too. The disconnect will bring up questions and challenges early on in your presentation, rather than waiting for a 'thank you' slide at the end and an awkward silence.

Room 2. In this group of content, Room 2 looks to draw out and explore the outcomes that will be achieved by the company's decision to take on your offer, and the negative or less desirable outcomes that will occur by buying someone else's product:

- The promise of how you can solve the challenges outlined in Room 1

- How this works in detail

- Data and financial calculations of alternative inferior outcomes

Room 3. This is where you prove that you can deliver on the promise made in Room 2. It's about demonstrating you are capable and have successfully delivered on the promise to other customers. Your goal is to build trust and reduce risk to make it easy to say yes:

- Evidence that you are the best choice

- Case studies

- Social proof

- How you will deliver

Room 3 is where most presentations start. After a brief intro, they go straight into why they're best placed to deliver, but they don't set the scene of the context. Many never even touch on either of the first two rooms.

What does this look like in practice? Here's a great example: imagine you're driving down the highway on a long journey with a quarter of a tank of fuel. You see a petrol station coming up and recognise the name. The prices look reasonable. Do you stop? You might, you might not. You believe this would be a fine place to fill up, but that's all. You only have the Room 3 evidence.

Now imagine the station gives you some context: it's the last one for ages! There are no other stations in the vast desert you have to cross after you pass it! The desert's uninhabited except for highly venomous scorpions! (As an Australian, this is the case way too often.) Now you have more information to make your decision. You understand the wider context of the world ahead of you, and the consequences you might face by not stopping here and taking the offer. You've been taken through rooms 1 and 2, and so now when you arrive at 3, you're desperate to buy from them.

By breaking and aligning the content like this, you can then walk your audience through each room in turn, transforming the information into a sales presentation format. In other words, it automatically becomes a strategic narrative of the overall concept that needs to be communicated. You give your audience more information to come to the decision you want them to take: to buy from you.

3. Storytelling – The Hero's Journey

Here, the basic structure is to follow the idea of an arc, where the engagement and conversion – the main drivers of the presentation – are woven into a narrative. When we talk about the hero's journey, it's a way of describing the progress of a story that has a main character as its lead. Mainly used in fiction, the idea of the arc can work in a presentation as well. The hero usually embarks on journey from their usual place in life and is then presented with a challenge. They then go on to encounter all kinds of obstacles, people and events that either help them or stop them from achieving their goal, always learning and becoming more enlightened along the way. At the high point of their adventure, the hero overcomes their greatest challenge, gains new knowledge (usually valuable) and goes back to their old world wiser, cleverer and with the ability to help others. (Think James Bond, although he usually receives a different kind of reward!)

A presentation follows a similar format in the form of an arc, and then concludes with new knowledge. It's a very handy metaphor when putting together a set of ideas that need to be engaging and interesting.

Who should be the lead character in your hero's journey? If it's not you, you can often bring a case study or use case to life by telling the story from the perspective of a user – covering how difficult their life was before your solution, discovering the 'secret' that changed things for them and ending wiser and happier.

4. Audience Guided – Conversational Presenting

One of the strongest appeals of using Prezi is the option to chart your own course as you present – you can decide on the order you present your content in based on a conversation with your audience in a live environment. It's an incredibly powerful and effective way of presenting that transforms a one-way presentation into a two-way conversation.

All the groups or topics can be seen on a home screen. Through engagement with your audience, you can decide on what topic to focus on and instantly access it. It's a fundamental shift from traditional presenting and can be incredibly effective. Improvements to PowerPoint have allowed Prezi-like features to be recreated. Rather than having a set of presentations, content can be collated into one master deck and designed with a home page to enable topic navigation with a click. (If you haven't seen this before, it might be hard to imagine so we've got a tutorial and example on the book's website: https://presentation-design.co/playbook.)

It's not that technically hard to create. The shift is to leave the traditional presentation approach of following a set path of groups and content to being able to move freely. The option for clients to choose their own adventure is unique, but it does need a certain amount of setup to make it run smoothly. If you've seen the examples, you can start to think about what parts of your presentation this can apply to.

- **Training presentations.** You can show all of the modules up on the home page and use that as an agenda to follow.

- **Product library.** You may have a sales presentation with multiple products. You can show all of these on one screen in a master presentation and simply click on what's needed at the time.

- **Case studies.** Part of your presentation may be linear, but you may work in different industries and client types. You can build a library of case studies and present them in this format so that during the presentations, you or the clients can choose the relevant ones to explore.

Can AI help you create a presentation?

This question is only going to become more prevalent as AI advances. My answer is already yes, absolutely, and you should be trying to use it. While not a perfect system, the research and writing ability of AI tools has significantly changed the way we approach content creation. As with all tools, this technology exists to assist in synthesising content, and is an enormously powerful tool that's incredibly useful for time management.

By giving prompts to an AI assistant (while making sure your references are in place), much-needed insights will happen very quickly. This really is a simple and relatable technique that is accessible to all. Get good at writing good prompts to help you with:

- Outline organisation

- Idea generation

- Slide heading ideas

- Relevant facts and data

To assist you further in this process, use a voice app such as Otter to record your ideas and then using AI, ask GPT to write a hundred words to get you started. As the tech is likely to change and improve very quickly, try to become skilled at creating great prompts to mine the most out of the tool.

Be aware that AI isn't there to create the presentation for you. It's your ideas, delivery and spontaneity that all contribute to make a compelling and memorable presentation. AI can simply take the hard, time-consuming parts away and give you suggestions.

How to transfer these structures to PowerPoint

Once you've decided on a structure, with the 5 Power Principles in mind, it's time to transfer these to PowerPoint.

Create sections

The very first task is to create a title slide. Once you have taken the content and created groups as described earlier, use the divider slides and think of them as chapter headings based on your groups of content. Give each section a name and this will immediately serve as the structure.

Now is the time to zoom out and take a first look at the big picture. That's the start of your framework and how your presentation can guide the audience to a new level of understanding.

Create slide headings

Begin assessing content for your sections and start by making meaningful headings. The linear nature of a slide progression tends to direct us to compartmentalise our thoughts and think of each slide as a separate idea. That's like trying to write a song note by note. A presentation is a journey through knowledge imparted in a smooth, digestible flow. We tend to think of slide headings as a three-to-five-word summary that can be seen on the screen.

A massively underused and highly effective technique is to embrace the titles of each slide and use those to support a compelling narrative in a conversational way. Then, as you review the flow of your deck, the headings join together to create a quick and engaging story. I try to aim for titles that contain around a dozen words in a conversational format. Each has a feature or benefit for your audience or sets up a context or question that you intend to address. When comparing the two examples of headings below, which type would you rather listen to?

	Usual headings	Powerful headings
Slide 1	About Us	In 1958, three engineers joined forces with a focus on precision.
Slide 2	Our Locations	Where clients exist, we put our team on the ground to support them.
Slide 3	The Team	A group of highly experienced, easy-to-work-with specialists.

Keep checking consistency and the all-important flow by zooming out and overviewing regularly. Is your presenter's intent still there? Move between sections as you need to; work through the slides from top to bottom and just read the headings. Does it all connect and make sense? If it does, you have achieved your goal.

The task is then to fill out as many of these slides as possible and keep scanning through them to check the flow. If you add more slides into the deck, carefully check that you are keeping with your original grouping and making sure each slide adds to your presentation. You don't want to just drop in random content out of order.

Follow the arc

Clear ideas and structures help you tell engaging stories that make your point.

Notice how I ditched the normal 'Just to note' heading here?

To effectively engage with your audience, you need to begin with an idea, create coherent content which boasts a natural arc and deliver that content in an engaging and effective manner. That's the way to guarantee your audience takes on board your message.

11
Develop Dynamic Content

You've chosen your structure and built the foundation of your presentation. Now comes the work to bring it to life with content that takes your audience on a journey to the destination you've planned for them. But you'll need to make sure the journey itself is an interesting one, or they'll never finish it.

The stakes just got higher

In looking to win the war for attention and make an impact, you now have to create and collate content, ideas, insights and data around each of the key groups of your presentation structure.

You've probably created countless presentations and gone through this step many times. If you follow the

5 Power Principles, you've got the right mindset to get there, but there's a fatal flaw that occurs at this stage: the content dump.

When you're deep into creating your content, it's so easy to get caught up and lose sight of the original goal of your presentation. You feel the temptation to add more and more detail, thinking that more is better. You start to turn inwards and forget about the needs of our audience and their mindset. This is the stage where you can lose connection. Even with the best intentions at the start, you can lose your way. The result? A presentation that you no longer feel great about and that no amazing design or delivery will fix.

This isn't about telling you what content you need to choose for your presentation. That's your job. Instead, what I want to show you is a framework and way of thinking that will guide you through the process and help you generate compelling content. It's a simple three-step checklist on what you should include and what you shouldn't. Then we'll spend a bit of time talking about some of the key ideas around the type of content you should be presenting.

Why presentation content fails

With so many variables, I've boiled down this advice to three simple measures. If each part of your presentation passes these checks, you'll be in good shape. This checklist comes from the main challenges around content that cause presentations to fail. It turns each of those into a guideline to give you clarity:

1. **Too much content.** Be relevant and precise; you need to be a judicious gatekeeper and warden and resist the 'everything' urge. Like a curator at a gallery, there's a reason and purpose for everything you've chosen to include and the integrity across the whole presentation is your role.

2. **Not easily understood.** Keep it simple and digestible. You need to keep in mind where your audience is in the world, their knowledge and perspective and how much of what you present they will understand. You are their guide.

3. **Not interesting enough.** Make it engaging – you have endless ways to share content. Your job isn't just to speak objectively to ideas, insights and information: your job is to do package them up in ways that amplify them.

Avoiding the pitfalls

From these three areas where presentation content often falls down, we can come up with three ways to avoid these pitfalls.

1. Be the gatekeeper

If you've created your presentation structure first, this should be an easier task. When a musician writes a song, they consider how the notes connect. When an author writes a book, they are mindful of the flow between pages. Similarly, in a presentation, it's your role to make sure that there's a logical flow to the content that you include. You can do this by thinking about the context of your content. Sure, slides are free, so it's easy to keep adding them, but should you be? Each time you want to include a new slide, look at the slides before and after. Ask yourself the questions:

- Does this make sense?

- Is there a logical progression from the slide I've just presented to what comes next?

- At the end of this slide, what will my audience be thinking before I start the next one?

- Is this important and necessary?

- If I take out this slide, will the overall presentation suffer? What is vital and what is fluff?

Start with the assumption that every slide should be in an appendix as a reference; only have it in your deck if it's vital. You will know you are on track when you feel that there is a plan as you review your deck. Aim for a smooth journey that keeps your audience on track for where you want to lead them and doesn't take unnecessary stops.

2. Make your message simple and digestible

Far too often, impact is lost when a presenter hasn't taken the time to think about how they communicate complex, technical or specialist topics. It creates a mess and puts the audience off; people don't like the feeling of not understanding.

At the other end of the spectrum, it's a deeply engaging process to watch someone who has embraced Power Principle #1 (The audience is number one). They have taken the time to think of their audience and they've done the work to make their content relatable and easy to understand.

Imagine you are speaking about blockchain, leadership strategy, or legislation changes. It would be easy to lose your audience if you weren't careful, right? So, break the essential components and make the basic information easy to understand. You don't want to oversimplify, merely aim for easy and digestible. One of the best ways to understand this is to model your approach on the experts.

Richard Feynman was a Nobel Prize-winning theoretical physicist responsible for reinventing quantum electrodynamics, which is the theory of the interaction between light and matter, and changed the way science now understands the nature of waves and particles. He was one of the greatest minds of his generation, but he didn't stand out because of what he knew.

He stood out from among other smart, accomplished people because of his communication style.

He was known as 'the great explainer' as he was able to take complex ideas and help people with non-scientific backgrounds understand and embrace them. His audience loved him for that. He made them feel smarter, empowered and more open to learning. This is exactly what you can do as a presenter.

Richard developed a very simple process to follow: a four-step mental model called the Feynman Technique. The essence was to understand all you know about a certain subject, including your own knowledge gaps, and then explain it to a twelve-year-old. By doing this, you aren't presenting *at* your audience, you are meeting them where they are and guiding them and, in the process, creating an amazing sense of engagement.

Look at what you're presenting and ask yourself, 'Is this the easiest way I can help my audience understand?' Go back to Power Principle #1. You don't want to ask your audience to make a big leap in what they understand or believe. That's a hard thing to ask. Instead, build a bridge to the new information you want your audience to learn. Take them step by step. You gain credibility and authenticity by making your audience understand and connect with what you are saying:

- Show yourself as an expert by being a great explainer.

- Remember the level of understanding will vary across your audience. Start with a base level to check in and then build into detail.

- Be humble and use easy to understand language and terms. When you start to introduce technical jargon or concepts, explain them as you go.

3. Create engaging content

You've already been a gatekeeper and adopted the mindset of being an explainer. Now you have to ensure the content in your presentation is engaging. A content dump isn't going to capture your audience's attention and win the war. You know this. Your role is to think about what you are really trying to achieve and find the best way to package it. Your audience will be a diverse group but what they have in common are some basic human characteristics:

- They hate boring and will quickly turn to autopilot if boredom kicks in.

- They will be able to remember more of something that has emotion attached to it.

- They value novelty, new things, learning things, 'aha' moments and a sense of surprise.

- Their brain likes a framework to remember facts, figures and ideas.

Six compelling ways to package your content

With this in mind, here are six effective ways to take what you'd like to present and package it into something compelling.

1. Use stories

We know the deal with stories: they're powerful because they allow us to connect emotionally on a personal level. The best stories are ones we can actually feel, both as a presenter and a human being. Why is this? Basically, it's because we all have a library of personal experiences that will resonate with your topic, and you can use those experiences to make your story shine.

Generally, when working with new clients, we see brand focused, brochure-type presentations that seriously lack connection, both with the material and the audience. Then, after some initial probing in an interview setting, clients often reveal a wealth of relevant and rich stories that were never included in their initial presentation.

Stories work very well as they make for interesting listening, the emotional aspect is easier to recall and they compel audiences to create a mental model. The great thing about them is they allow the presentation tempo to lead up to a change that may ruffle a few feathers, which is good for embedding a message and makes you more relatable.

The term 'corporate storytelling' may not sound appealing as it can feel manufactured or inauthentic, but it is invaluable for audience engagement. You want to ensure the stories you use don't come across as fake or overly high-level so as not to lose your audience's interest. There's also the risk of telling stories that are irrelevant or awkward. You can be personal and reveal yourself, but not without a reason, and not without double-checking you'd be happy for that same story to be repeated without you there.

Look at the content you have right now. Below is a checklist of the types of stories to use:

- **Customer stories.** How are people using your product or service? Narrow the story down so you're talking about a specific long-term, disgruntled, active or lost customer. They don't have to be a paying customer – just someone who's used or experienced your offer.

- **Context stories.** This is where you can find a parallel between your content and a comparable scenario. To help the acceptance of a new product, service or way of thinking, share the story of a different industry, team or technology that is comparable and has been successful.

- **Origin stories.** These show the 'why' in a certain way of doing things. Where did the need originate from; why do you believe something to be true; why is something so important to you? What's in the past that will inform the ideas in this presentation?

- **Perspective stories.** A beautiful way of helping share an idea is to look at the same thing from the lens of different people. Looking to lead a team to solve a complex problem? Examine its impact and the challenge from two, three or even four different views. This is a wonderful sense of exploration that encourages your audience to think deeper.

- **Future scenario stories.** How will people use what you are presenting in the future? What impact will it have? Rather than talking through an adaptation of a new service or product in numbers and percentages, wind the clock forwards. Set a date. Share what that future will look like then.

Stories can be fifteen seconds or twenty minutes; it is up to you to work through them. Check to see what you have that will inform your audience.

2. Share case studies

Case studies are an enormously powerful way of reducing complexity. They are relatable, interesting and demonstrate concrete evidence of the impact by showing the before and after of the topic.

Have you ever seen a presentation where the presenter admits their product or service doesn't work, is too expensive or has failed for clients? Or is it more common that they present their product as a wonderful solution that will benefit all? My guess is you'll usually witness the latter. It would be fair to point out that your audience will naturally be sceptical of such claims. We often see presenters undermine their presentations by failing to acknowledge this scepticism and neglecting to substantiate their claims with examples from real-life clients.

If you can't prove what you're saying is real, then stop and ask yourself if there's any chance your audience will believe you. An authentic, real-life client use case will win over fake ones every time. Share how transformational the offer is rather than relying on just facts; illustrate an idea by using actual case studies to support your evidence.

If you are concerned about confidentiality, you can pre-empt this and arrange a consultation and signoff with clients to get their permission. You can also redact details or generalise to a point where it's not identifiable. If it's public information, make sure to note that and the source so you can freely share. Try using one of the case studies below if you need inspiration:

- **Comparison case study.** Develop a case study with a before/after or a side-by-side comparison of how things were before the relationship with your offering and reveal the resulting world. Then draw the before and after to a close with a comparison. You can still use numbers and percentages, but now they show the difference with a guided understanding.

- **'A day in the life'.** If you ever feel you get stuck in the details of explaining a product or concept that has multiple applications or is technically challenging, change your perspective and narrate the step-by-step of how people use it. Go from start to finish through a person's day. Spend the time to make it feel real and easy to understand. The key to 'day in the life' case studies is making them feel authentic. Use interesting names. Make good use of places and dates as tools that add to the study's realness.

3. Develop models and processes

In modelling and processing, a lot can be shown in PowerPoint around steps, sequences and the technique of undertaking a task with a view to a result. Instead of just listing them, think about how it's done and create a wrapper by allocating a name to the process or way of thinking. For example, instead of offering your audience five generic bullet points, give them a label and make them proprietary. Call it 'The XYZ Way of Project Management' or 'The ABC Method'. This simple change gives the audience a structure to embrace and use in their own modelling. The design section will cover what to do with these processes and models for visual economy, but for now, think about what you can do to make them stand out.

4. Explain data

Numbers and data in the form of charts or graphics act as evidence of a claim. If you've followed the processes so far, you should have a great title on your slide that links your flow, and your data evidence will relate to and support that. Most of the data within charts can be improved visually and impactfully with standout design, although in presenting numbers and data there can be two big challenges: millions and billions, and trends and time.

Millions and billions: The brain isn't perfect at appreciating numbers without context. One of the reasons for that is that big numbers, like 1 billion, don't take up that much space when written down. Even the sounds don't vary all that much: million, billion, trillion.

This raises the alarm when you're trying to make the message about values or amounts sink in. If the design around number stats is poor, your audience will lose the sense of scale or miss the impact. So, when using numbers, you want to look for ways to bring them to life in a relative way that can easily be understood. Here are two examples.

1. The first showcases scale you can visualise:
   'We delivered a sustainability program that has
   led to a 9% increase in recycling of office plastic,'
   can be replaced by, 'We've delivered a sustainability program that's stopping eight Olympic
   pools of plastic from being dumped into landfill
   every day.'

2. The second looks at opportunity cost: 'Without
   further action and advocacy, we are looking
   at a budget reduction of 3%,' can be replaced
   by, 'Without further action and advocacy, we
   will lose funding equivalent that supports over
   450 students.'

The difference is pretty clear!

Trends and time: In reality, change or implementa-
tion of substantial processes or infrastructure moves
slowly. You need to find ways to make the data stand
out regardless. For instance, to show a slower progression, draw out the outcome by displaying a variety
of future periods with comparative graphics. Doing
this brings the future into the present for the audience
and gives a feeling of reality. Combine it with a metaphor and you have a very powerful way of creating
an impact.

Here's an example of how rethinking stats can have
an impact: Susan is a HR Manager at a large training

company who receives student feedback on course effectiveness. She's presenting at the monthly executive update on facilitators' performance. Over the last period, their score has dropped from an average of 9.4/10 to 8.5. Student satisfaction is down 9.6%.

Presented that way, it doesn't look too scary – but there is a trend. The problem with trends is they may not receive enough attention as they're not an emergency... Yet. Let's look at presenting this another way, ignoring the <10% decrease in satisfaction and looking instead at the growth of dissatisfaction: student dissatisfaction is up 250% (from 0.6 to 1.5).

See the difference? Now that's a panic-worthy headline. When you want to make an impact with small numbers, look for growth or a gap. Illustrate what cost savings would mean for the business. For example, if the cost saving is out there and has yet to be located or emphasised, spotlight it. This creates impact and emphasises trends rather than finality and lack of progression.

5. Generate questions

You can do anything with a great question. Questions can be a bridge, a pause or a way to create engagement. They can be used to take your audience down different paths, or add a voice of dissent when emphasising a point. Questions are a brilliant way of switching the mental energy back to the audience and making them think.

You can get away with just about anything when it's phrased as a question. When an aspect of the topic doesn't seem to fit, a pointed question can create a bit of controversy. It can be a device to set up a scenario or explore a new idea.

Questions also serve to create a sense of unfolding and intrigue to lead an audience. Use them. They are wonderful and can be open, rhetorical or guided. You decide. Here are some examples:

- Why would people use us?

- What would happen if...?

- If we aren't going to solve this, who is?

- What's better, option A or B?

- Should we look to do this? Why or why not?

- What would our closest competitor do?

- What do you think would happen if...?

- Does anyone know what the most important part of X is?

- What would so-and-so think about this?

- If we look to the future, what do we see?

- Can we take a moment to reflect?

Does reading this list trigger some powerful ways you can use questions? It's good to be aware that you know where you are taking your question, and how to make the answer work to open paths of communication. This helps to illuminate the answers you receive from the audience.

6. Share social proof

An easy to create but often forgotten way to make content compelling is to show evidence that what you're saying is actually true. You will find that letting other people be your advocates can be incredibly powerful. It shows real evidence that people are saying good things about you. This tack allows you to step aside, be humble and let real-life people say it for you. Social proof is showing your audience a summary of the desired impact with testimonials, names, even words from the clients themselves.

What to do when you get stuck

Making an impact relies on clear, organised thoughts and requires a streamlined approach on the part of the presenter. That's really hard to do when it's 4:58pm and you are six meetings into the day with a full inbox. Just sitting at your workspace, a table or a desk isn't where breakthroughs and creative ideas arrive.

There can be so much visual processing and so many thoughts in your head that there isn't space for good ideas. Plus, distractions abound and clearing your inbox feels easier.

When you get stuck, you need to make progress. If you've just been given a whole heap of content and need to work out a way to organise it, get outside for a walk. Find your walking spot, get out and go.

Press reset. Left foot, right foot. History is full of famous walkers; Steve Jobs discovered long strolls worked for him, and Churchill… Well, Churchill liked to take a bath. At least he got away from the office!

New science is showing the power the sun has to release cortisol and the effects on the brain and lateral eye movement. Plus, it's great to help block out the noise. Take the pressure off yourself. Put your phone away and listen to music (not a podcast – you're making room for inspiration, so that needs some mental space).

Provide that space, but look out for the moment inspiration hits and don't lose it. It's a small, fragile space where those new ideas suddenly flash through. It may be a word or a way to display content, a way to introduce an idea or a memory of something you've seen that you'd like to incorporate.

Just to note

Be picky with what content you include, and your audience will thank you for it. Stick to the essential info to build your flow. Then consider what you have at your disposal. Look for ways to engage your audience among the stories, questions, proof and data that will hammer home your message.

12
Design Distinctive Visuals

Your goal with this step is to create a visual aid that looks professional and supports your presentation. This doesn't require you to be a professional designer, though. With some simple techniques, you can elevate your deck and increase your impact. I'm going to throw a lot of tips at you over the next few pages, so it's up to you to take the useful parts and apply them to your own presentations.

Visuals matter

Businesses and organisations spend a lot of effort and invest huge amounts of money on their appearance and the parts of their business that customers interact with. Huge buildings with logos on them, websites that look amazing with teams of people supporting them and campaigns that cost millions of dollars. They want to appear professional and capable and to stand out.

However, clients – typically important, high-value clients – often interact with a particular touch point which regularly lets businesses down. Of course, we're talking about the quality of their presentation decks. It's not uncommon for visuals to ruin presentations.

Think about some of the presentations that you might have seen in the past few years. Have they been clean, fresh, visually appealing presentations that help support the presenter? Or is it more likely that you've seen your fair share of a mix of jumbled formatting and slide after slide of text?

I get to review hundreds of presentations decks a year across a huge range of industries, from start-ups to global brands. Despite what's at stake for the presenters, the decks are letting them down and reducing the chance of them making an impact time and time again. It's a problem and a weakness where one of the most personal and high-touch communication assets consistently doesn't match and live up to other assets in the business. There are two root causes of this.

1. **Most presenters aren't designers.** This means they struggle with branding, design and

formatting. If you want to establish credibility with your audience and be seen as a professional presenter, slides with a mix of random font sizes, colours and pixelated, outdated stock images won't cut it.

2. **Slides aren't speaking notes.** It's too easy to write out your slides with what you want to say. So rather than using your slides as a visual aid to enhance your message, they become the sole focus of your audience. If they're concentrating on reading a text-dense slide, they aren't focusing on you. This kills engagement and reduces your chance of having an impact.

As a result, most presentations appear as what we call a Frankendeck – a mish-mash collection of slides pulled from five other decks over time and pasted together with eight different types of formatting, outdated imagery, pages of bullet points and branding that only slightly resembles its original theme. You can't be an impactful presenter if you are using a Frankendeck. You might be an authentic presenter who has rehearsed and is ready to deliver but if you're using high school formatting and a jumbled Frankendeck of slides, you instantly lose credibility and the ability for your slides to support your delivery.

To win the war for attention and make an impact, it's time to decide to cut away from the ordinary and make the commitment to doing something better.

You can fix your Frankendeck

At Presentation Design Co, we specialise in creating Tier 1 presentations for clients. These are clean, modern, high-impact presentations that cut through and make an impact. They represent the top 10% of presentations used throughout the world. From conferences to sales presentations to investor updates, they make a massive difference in helping clients achieve their goals. It's transformational for them. With a team of world-class, highly experienced presentation specialists, it's a level of presentation that we are able to consistently create and guarantee as an outcome to clients.

If you are creating your own presentation, challenge yourself to do the same: aim for Tier 1. While this might sound beyond you, the good news is that since most presentations are so low quality, even simple improvements can dramatically improve the quality of the slides that you present with, better engage your audience and boost the impact you have.

Very soon, AI tools will take up the slack of design for you. However, there are very simple things you can do to fix your presentation slides that don't require much time or technical knowledge. Simply making them less of an eyesore is an efficient proposition that will instantly lift your deck above the millions of other ones being worked on. Nail these and you will upskill yourself to iron out the inconsistencies of a Frankendeck without having to become a presentation designer.

Four elements of presentation design

Let me break down the four elements of presentation design and what you can do to fix your Frankendeck in each. It's going to be hard to see the visual transformation this creates in a book. If you'd like to see the step-by-step process, you can follow it in the website accompanying the book, where we have tutorials and downloadable assets for each step: https://presentationdesign.co/playbook.

1. Set and follow a consistent branding and theme

These are the brand elements of fonts and colours that you have to work with, either from a PowerPoint template or corporate guidelines. It's the consistent use of these guidelines across a presentation that make a big difference to its overall impact.

The first thing is to be aware of what sits on your Master Slide versus what you can see on the screen. If you are working from a template, it can be a frustrating experience seeing an element on screen and then not being able to edit it. Take a moment and go to 'View Master' in PowerPoint. This will show you the entire range of elements that you have to work with.

If you need to make universal changes to your deck, this is where it can take place. It will have the wireframe of what you are working on.

Start with fonts. The first place to start fixing your Frankendeck is your fonts. Great font choice with a consistently applied weight makes a huge improvement in any deck.

A significant factor historically holding back slides has been the need for the use of corporate PowerPoint fonts like Calibri and Arial that were universally available. Fonts and typography are a core ingredient of great design. Brands like Audi and Rolex are recognisable from their consistent use of elegant, distinctive fonts, yet other companies with amazing brands were having to stick to 'safe', plain, widely used fonts so that they could avoid formatting problems.

Now, PowerPoint allows users to embed the fonts they use into presentations. It's a feature that unlocks the power of typography and provides a huge degree of flexibility in the way it's used.

Find the right one. Your brand guidelines will show you what to use. If you have free choice, you can either use font families or font pairs.

- **Font families:** Most fonts have a 'family' that includes variable thicknesses of the same font. As with size, we typically use bold for headings, semi-bold for subheadings and regular for body copy. You can vary font weight along with size to establish a content hierarchy.

- **Font pairs:** Like food and wine, combining two fonts together can look great and give the text on your slide a natural hierarchy. You simply choose two complementary fonts and set them together.

We would recommend. Should you use default fonts or Google some fonts? If you want to stick to the safest option, try these two combinations in PowerPoint:

- Headings – Barlow Condensed
- Body – Montserrat

You can also download and install a number of Google fonts online. We would recommend trying:

- Headings – Lora
- Body – Source Sans Pro

Set and follow some rules. Now you have your fonts decided, it's important to set yourself some rules and follow them throughout. This is a key building block that you'll repeat to build your deck. As an example:

- Headings: Bold in size 30 – Black
- Subheadings: Semi-bold in size 18 – Brand colour
- Body copy: Light in size 12 – Dark grey

You can go back to update the template. Be aware of any text that has been entered, as the manual text box won't be updated. This will be a slightly tedious step, but worth the time. Go to each slide, check the settings and update text as needed. From here, all you need to is make sure you use these new settings. If you are pasting in new content, select 'paste to match style' to make imported text match the new setting.

2. Establish a hierarchy to show what's important

From a design perspective, the 'success test' for each slide has two steps. The first is the 'gist' test – when you first see a slide on the screen, in the first two to three seconds, can you scan it and immediately get an initial understanding of what it's communicating? The second is that after you have the 'gist', can you easily follow a natural order of what to read and process?

You can increase the impact of your slides by understanding the importance of laying out content to give a hierarchy. Hierarchy in the context of design is the visual organisation of elements in a layout. Each element has its own relative importance, which is reflected through position, size, contrast and colour.

The challenge with most decks is that there is a mismatch. Over 80% of slides we see simply follow the suggested PowerPoint template layout options. They're easy to use as a starting point but aren't designed to provide the best impact for your content.

'Cookie cutter' layouts don't help you create the hierarchy you need to emphasise your key points. There are three ways you can visually establish a hierarchy on your slides:

- **Size.** We all know a heading should be the largest component compared to subheadings and body copy. This also applies to the size of shapes, diagrams and images. For example, a pricing table typically has the most popular or recommended option in the biggest box; it's instantly obvious this is the option the business wants you to focus on. The most important content on your slide should be the biggest in comparison to other content.

- **Position.** In English, we read from left to right, so it's important to follow that natural instinct when you have a lot of information on a slide. When we format content in a bulleted list, we read it from top to bottom, assuming the first point is the most important. But what we can aim for is to create a good balance.

- **Space.** When you want to show that something's important, give it space! A key point shouldn't be surrounded by other distractions. The cornerstone message of your presentation can have its own slide. A graph that needs to be shown in detail can't be crammed alongside three others. Use of space will lead you to bold, uncluttered slides that catch your audience's eye.

3. Creative visualisation

Slides exist to support a presentation and the temptation is to just write our speaking notes in them. Even those of us who realise the folly in this might at least jot some bullet points down to remind ourselves of our next idea. But here's a painful truth: *bullet points reduce your effectiveness.*

I understand this may be upsetting news. Many of you reading this will be staunch supports of the 'bullet point list' style of presenting. I don't want your whole world view to come crashing down. But I'm asking you to approach this with an open mind – I'm on your side and it's time to accept that bullet points don't work.

How our brains react to text-heavy presentation slides has been studied and brilliantly explained by Australian neuroscientist Dr Jared Cooney Horvath. He tells us how both sides of our brain contain an auditory cortex that pulls in all the sounds we hear, including the tone, pace and inflection of someone's voice.

In a presentation, the auditory cortex picks up the sounds of the speaker's voice. These then travel to the parts of the brain where the processing and comprehension of what the speaker is saying takes place. What's interesting is that these areas are only capable of comprehending one voice at a time. Although we can hear lots of voices at once, a part of our brain called the left inferior frontal gyrus acts as a gateway, allowing only one voice to pass through for comprehension.

If we have two people speaking to us at once, we can only focus on one for comprehension. Although we can *hear* the other voice, we never really process it; it gets ignored. We might think of reading as a silent exercise, but it's not. When we read a line of text, we do it using a voice in our head (mostly our own), and this is picked up by our auditory cortex.

Therein lies the problem.

When a presenter is using text-heavy slides *and* speaking, we have two inputs – their voice, plus the voice in our head as we read through the slides. Both voices are competing to be let in for processing, but only one can get through; the other will be ignored and disappear. When this happens throughout multiple presentation slides, we're constantly switching between our reading voice and the speaker's voice, which makes the brain feel exhausted and reduces the quality of both inputs.

What's the solution? *Seven.*

It's been determined that seven words or less don't create a conflict in your brain. It's short enough for us to quickly parse, and our processing areas aren't activated by images, so the speaker's voice will travel through without distraction. A text-light, more visual approach helps you as an aid that doesn't compete with what you're saying.

There are four ways you can transform your text-heavy slides. If we're not using bullet points to format our key talking points, what are our options? Ultimately, we want to move away from a 'top to bottom' list and use as much real estate on the slide as possible. This creates a more balanced layout and hierarchy of content. Reformat the text. If there's a reason you can't remove text from your slide, then it's about improving the layout of what's on screen.

1. Break it up. You can use horizontal or vertical lines to create visual dividers between related content. This is a clean and simple way to help an audience absorb information by establishing a structure and hierarchy. It's a great way to lift the look of a layout without taking up too much space. Boxes help create a layout that looks balanced and shows clear separation, as well as a hierarchy of content.

By grouping your content in these containers, you're improving the impact of the reading experience for the audience and the overall design aesthetic. When using boxes, it's important to maintain alignment. Boxes should be aligned from top to bottom and left to right, with an equal distance in between. You can then bold out the most important parts of each sentence to give variety and add focus to what's most important.

2. Keywords and icons. Pull out keywords from each sentence that gives your audience the gist of what you're saying. Teaming that with a simple and relevant icon as a visual anchor provides context and tone to your keywords. This allows you to talk freely about your key points. It's less overwhelming and far more impactful.

3. Replace text with images. Choosing images for the sake of it isn't the most effective way to create impact. If you do use imagery, I'd recommend avoiding images that are irrelevant, garish or look like stock images. You know the ones we're talking about: the row of corporate people standing with thumbs up. Or those weird 'blob men' you might have come across on stock image websites. And when we want to be *really* creative, we try to be metaphorical, yet highly clichéd – the puzzle piece, the tip of the iceberg, climbing the mountain. It's all been seen and done before.

Images should, first and foremost, support your content – not detract from it. It's easy to rip off low-quality, low-resolution images from Google, but they make a presentation look cheap and tacky, the very opposite of how you want to present yourself (sophisticated and professional). Instead, you want authentic images that aren't overly posed or edited. The people in them should look like regular people doing regular things – especially a diversity of people that feels balanced, not forced.

It's also great when you have a theme to help keep things consistent: cityscapes, epic landmarks, lifestyle or casual office people. To further help with consistency, you can find talented photographers with libraries on Shutterstock, Getty, etc. They each have a distinct style, with image categories depending on the topic. Or, if you have the time and budget, consider hiring a photographer to take photos of your office, team, facilities, clients, etc. It's the highest form of authenticity and a worthwhile investment.

When searching for images, the key is to not be too specific with terms such as 'man in a suit at the office', which will limit your search. Be open to options and search using general terms such as, 'office people', 'epic landscapes' or 'drone nature' – some of our go-to searches. You can also explore libraries or collections on sites like Unsplash, a free image website. Make sure you have a theme in mind for your search.

4. Use charts and diagrams to show data, trends and proportions visually. The golden rule for charts is 'Clean and simple always wins'. It's no secret that default charts and graphs in PowerPoint – or even in general – aren't sexy. Their main function is to communicate data. But when data is presented in a poor format, it's uninspiring, doesn't feel sophisticated and isn't as impactful as it could be. As a result, the audience either needs to work hard to decipher the information, or they'll simply switch off.

When you add charts and diagrams, avoid the default look and feel by editing the style. Tweaking charts and diagrams can make all the difference between looking like a basic PowerPoint and a professional infographic. If you want to come across as credible, reliable and professional, then clean, easy-to-read charts and graphs are a must.

Use brand colours – ideally, secondary colours from the brand palette. Create depth using drop shadows. Make sure they're light and subtle, with blur and light opacity so they don't feel too harsh. You can include curved borders for a softer look by adding a border and setting the cap type to 'round'. If these sound like technical changes beyond your IT capabilities, don't worry. They're easy to find from the Chart Design and Format menus in PowerPoint.

4. Look to create a visual impact

Impact is the overall impression and, hopefully, the 'wow' feeling that your audience has. It isn't one thing, it's the combination of your design coming together over the course of the presentation. But it definitely isn't spinning animation or dissolving elements – I can tell you that for certain.

Mix things up by making and breaking patterns. Our brain is wired to find and identify patterns. When it's in the process of trying to find them, the neocortex is busy and engaged. When you've seen seven identical layouts of slides in a row, you know what comes next, so the anticipation drops off.

By understanding this you can review your slides to look at repeated layout patterns – then break them. You don't need every slide to be different – things can feel jumbled that way. Instead, just make sure that you don't use the same layout for more than three to four slides. Feel free to mix things up and keep your audience engaged.

Save your audience from information overwhelm. Imagine this book had been written with no chapters, no breaks and no headings. Would you have made it this far? I wouldn't expect so. The standard practice of lining up content-heavy slides back-to-back isn't how our brain likes to follow and absorb information. This linear approach creates overwhelm to the point where our brains have had enough and shut off.

To make an impact, you need to leave enough space for the audience to digest and process what's being presented.

I mentioned earlier that we like to make each presentation into a story that seamlessly flows from slide to slide. Every story has chapters – natural breaks to let the reader know it's time to move to a different part of the same story. Instead of chapters, we use divider slides – a visual index to the key content groupings.

Typically, at the beginning of a presentation, you might see an agenda that highlights the topics to be covered, only to see it once and never revisited. We then forget about it and it's hard for our audience to follow the chapters without being reminded.

Make it easy for the audience to follow what you're saying – what you've already covered and what's still to come. Create a seamless user experience. By using divider slides, you're giving your audience a chance to reset and prepare for the next phase. The divider slide design can be simple, with just text, or you can take the opportunity to be more creative by using an image, graphics or even a video as a background.

Utilise transitions and animations. Our eyes are naturally attracted to movement. We find it interesting. The key to create something with impact in PowerPoint is to make sure it's with purpose and not distracting. Chequerboard transitions and bouncing text are just gimmicks. Instead try:

- **Click to fade in:** The simplest form of animation is still incredibly effective and easy to add. If your slide has a lot of content, choose two to three groups and add this animation. Set the duration to about two seconds so it doesn't feel rushed.

- **Push transitions:** Another easy to use and impactful technique is the push transition between slides. This creates a smooth connection to join slides and can be used very effectively when there's content between the slides that you'd like to connect.

- **Morph:** This is an amazingly underused feature that should be a must in your toolkit. If you'd like to create an animated movement between two slides, add the morph transition between the two and you'll be amazed by how interesting this can look. It's got lots of applications, so is worth spending the time to explore.

Just to note

Your presentation gets its first opportunity to grab your audience's attention with its title slide. Take this chance! From then on, avoid overwhelming them with text-heavy slides and instead complement what you're saying with strong visual aids.

13
Deliver With Confidence

The more prepared you are, the less nervous you should be. But, just in case, there are strategies to help prevent panic. The goal is to deliver with confidence as an engaging presenter in a face-to-face or online environment. It's not about not being nervous; it's about handling your nerves.

Nervous is natural

Believe me: even the most accomplished presenters feel nervous. The major contributor to feeling nervous during a presentation is the unknown. When we don't know what to expect in a live presentation environment, we're going to be in the spotlight, encountering factors we perceive as outside of our control. It could be a new location, a new audience or our first time presenting a topic. We're going to be judged; this is an important moment. All these feelings run contrary to our instinctive need to feel safe and protected. No wonder even starting to think about it makes us nervous.

The average presenter wants to seek comfort or feels unnecessarily overconfident, so they avoid the situation completely until the last minute. They feel safer by just turning up on the day and working it out when they're forced to be in the moment – aka the 'winging it' strategy – leaving it all to chance. This is a pretty popular corporate pastime, and I'm sure it's used around the world. You'd have seen enough of these presentations to know it's not an effective strategy.

In the world of professional presenters, speakers can be paid $5,000, $10,000 or $20,000 for a forty-five-minute slot. They're experts in preparing, with highly developed content, but often present at brand-new locations. At these price points, they're expected to deliver to the highest level every single time. From experience, they know the big barrier they face is the transition to get started and establish their flow. Once they're up and running, they can focus on the audience and presentation.

What we've observed over time is that these presenters are able to deliver and keep improving every presentation because:

- **They have a process.** They create confidence in their delivery by undertaking specific rituals and steps *before* their presentation. They don't wait until they're in the moment to react and work out what they're doing. They work proactively and rigorously to prepare before the presentation. This builds a steady confidence in them.

- **They can amplify their presence.** Great presenters know that their connection with an audience comes from a combination of factors: how they look, how they move and how they use their voice, and they have specific strategies to enhance all of these when delivering.

Let's look at how you can do the same.

The secret of the launch sequence

Have a process by developing a launch sequence.

A launch sequence is a checklist of actions that you can undertake in the leadup and start of your presentation. Rather than being at the mercy of all the unknowns and variables of presenting bouncing around your head, you take control by executing a series of predetermined, familiar actions.

By following a launch sequence, you feel comfortable and in control by acting to reduce anxiety and nerves. You'll have started with great momentum and in a much better position to successfully step into and deliver the body of the presentation. Depending on your presentation's size and scale, you can add in the steps you need, but here's a sample launch sequence:

- **One day before.** Technical details, event familiarisation and rehearsals should all be done. You should have an idea of logistics and be able to visualise the room, audience and setting in your head while having a checklist of practical details like a clicker and software updates.

  Decide what to wear. Picture yourself wearing it; visualise the moment. Set up for the next day by staying away from alcohol, sad movies and true crime podcasts. You want a clear, happy mind and a good night's sleep!

- **The morning of the presentation.** Set up your day with a positive intention. Do whatever you normally do to relax. Exercise, have breakfast, play happy music, meditate. Let yourself get in the zone and avoid being disturbed or distracted.

- **One hour before.** Try to be at the venue, or logged in to your presentation's platform, so you can enter the world you're going to present in. Switch off mentally from the outside world and turn off notifications and reminders to eliminate distractions.

- **Ten minutes to go.** Set your physiology to be fully present. This is usually when peak anxiety can strike. Remind yourself the work is done, and it's now time to focus completely on your audience. Work on your breathing, positive visualisation and shifting to your presentation persona. Smile, generate energy and make sure everything's in place. Understand the energy in the room, or if you're online, what your audience's mindset is.

- **One minute.** A moment of calm. This is a stage of complete focus and control, a mindset of blocking out thoughts and complete immersion in your surroundings. The goal here is to get out of your head and place yourself in the moment. Give yourself physical prompts of movement and balance to remind your body to keep moving. Keep it light and positive. Make yourself smile and feel the positive emotion. Sip some water. Remind yourself that the hard work is behind you with the preparation you've done.

- **Ten seconds.** The moment of connection and take-off. You've done the work of having a clear opening that addresses three aspects of your presentation – we'll cover this in detail in a separate part. Your goal is to confidently and calmly deliver what you've practised. You know what to say and how to say it.

Hopefully it's clear how, by breaking up your preparation into discrete phases, you can ensure you do the right actions at the right time to get yourself ready to deliver with confidence.

Capture the audience's attention

Given the challenge of intense competition, YouTubers have worked out the formula for capturing attention. With only a thumbnail and the first five to seven seconds of video as the window to win viewers over, they've become masters of the craft. A quick scroll through YouTube's daily top videos will show dozens of great examples.

In a presentation, as much as your audience would like to scroll past you to watch MrBeast, they can't. They are forced to give you at least some attention; you have very little competition after all. Don't be complacent. Understand that even if they are looking at you, your audience isn't 'with you' yet. Their minds are working through the email that just popped up, the meeting they have after watching you and dozens of things on their to-do list that aren't done, but need to be.

The first sixty seconds

To start with, you need to start strong. So, within the first sixty seconds, here are some things your audience probably won't be too inspired by hearing:

- 'We've got a lot to cover, so let me get into it quickly.'

- 'Is this working? Can you hear me?'

- 'Let's cover some housekeeping rules.'

Those first sixty seconds of a presentation are an amazing opportunity to capture the attention of your audience, set up a framework for your presentation and have the audience 'get you'. This is where they'll make their initial judgement on whether the exchange you're offering for their attention is something they are interested in taking.

The standard practice of most presentations is to copy the same safe and easy to say, pleasantly boring introductions that lack inspiration. As a result, audiences regularly encounter the same starts to a presentation: a stammered apology, regurgitating a LinkedIn bio, reading word by word off the agenda slide or, 'I'm so excited to be here today.' They aren't all terrible, but at the same time, they aren't that effective.

So, take a moment to think about your audience. High-impact, effective presenters labour over the first sixty seconds of a presentation incessantly because they know exactly what's at stake. You've heard the clichés around only having one chance to create a first impression. With presentations, as it's a deeper level of potential engagement, there's even more going on than that. If you miss this window, it is possible to win back an audience, but it's incredibly hard and starting strong is a much easier way to create an impact.

In the first sixty seconds, high-impact presenters do three things to set a successful foundation of delivery that you can use as a guide to starting strong: nail the intro, give a preview, and create an emotional connection.

1. Nail the intro

Unless you have to, the general advice is to skip the well-worn niceties and get straight into using a high-impact first line that helps you nail the introduction. Some of the ways of doing this:

- Share a compelling and contrasting view of the world: 'We are living in the most exciting time to be alive,' or, 'In twelve years, AI will kill your industry.'

- Ask a series of framing questions to set up your topic: 'Do we really know what it means to have a work/life balance? Have we been looking at this the right way and asking the right questions?'

- Say something shocking but relevant: 'Research shows that two-thirds of your staff probably really don't like their job or you.'

- Dive straight into a story that sets up a context of what you are: 'Just over two years ago, I woke up thinking it was going to be a regular Tuesday at the office. It wasn't. What happened that day changed my life; I just didn't know it at the time.'

- If that's too personal, tell the story of a staff member, a customer or an ex-customer, but share it from their perspective.

- Do something completely unexpected – be funny, dramatic and different. Break the pattern of 'regular' and signal to your audience that this will be unlike what they've seen before and thus worthy of their attention.

Whatever you choose for your opening, workshop it. Test it, try it. Make a moment of magic and build on it. Give people an immediate reason to come with you. Think about this as a mixture of alignment and interest. *Let's come to the same place together.* Lead the way.

2. Give a preview

Clearly communicate the value of the exchange by giving a preview. Unless you are giving a narrative keynote presentation (that really is just a long story), you should be working early on to give your audience a clear preview of what you are talking about and why it's compelling. People will be making a judgement if it's worth investing more of their attention, so work hard to make it interesting.

You can call this a benefit summary, outcome over-view, the payoff, the 'what's in it for me'... Call it whatever you want, frankly. Just make sure you know what it is and put it front and centre early on.

It's all about stacking up what's in the exchange to make it seem not just fair, but compelling. Setting the scene is really about being contextually aware of when you present.

Thinking about this now, right upfront, will influence your ideas and thinking throughout the whole of your presentation. It then becomes a guide for the relevance of your content and the order it should follow.

3. Create an emotional connection

I've referenced it many times: one of the judgements that people will form very early on is whether or not they like you. They don't have to like you for you to make an impact, but it often helps! This judgement doesn't take sixty seconds either; it's a snap judgement.

Like any group of people, you won't win everyone over, but when people make their judgement, do the work to make sure it's a fair reflection of you. Make sure you set out your presentation persona and lean into it. Do the work to be a real human being.

Another way to think of it is avoiding harming your chances of success by steering clear of any pet hates: don't be patronising, boring, arrogant, cocky, bland, cold, fake or seen to be trying too hard. These will absolutely sabotage your ability to form an emotional connection with your audience.

If you don't know where to start, just be personable and professional.

Follow the sequence

Once you've successfully hit the one minute mark, and have followed the 5 Principles, you've overcome the hardest part; now all that's left is the actual work of doing what you've planned to do. Follow your launch sequence and you'll have created a routine that conquers your nerves, puts you in control and sets you up to create an amazing engagement and impact.

Amplify your presence. We've already talked about creating a presentation persona – you, but a little bit *more*. Now it's time to dig into how you can put that presence to work as you present.

Supercharge your voice. When it comes time to present, yes, there are visuals and content, but it's the auditory component that is underrated and powerful. Great presenters know this and use their voice as a sharp weapon to make an impact. If you've done your preparation and are confident in the moment, it's your voice that is your magic instrument to play with.

Learning to harness it during your presentation will give you a secret superpower that will boost your confidence. For now, these are some ideas that you can use straight away:

Find your range. Think about each aspect of your voice as having a dial from the lowest setting of one to the highest of ten. Your job is to explore and find what that range looks like so when it comes to presenting, you are thinking about these variables objectively and looking to hit a number.

Then find your pitch. This is your ability to vary your voice from high to low, like musical notes. A continuous, flat monotone is hard to listen to and kills engagement. When talking 'to' a group, it's an easy trap to fall into as you aren't getting the usual responses, the back and forth and the pauses that you'd have in a conversation. Varying your pitch injects emotion into what you are saying and helps the audience better understand the meaning of the words being used.

Here's a practice sentence to try out modulating your pitch and the impact it has. Try reading aloud this quote from activist Malala Yousafzai: 'I raise up my voice – not so that I can shout, but so that those without a voice can be heard.'

Now find your 1, the lowest note. Dive *deep* down there. Ramp it up, explore, see where the 4 or 5 is, and work your way up to a 9. How does that feel? When you present, what needs to be a 3? Or a 7?

Use pace for emphasis. When we speak quickly, we can increase the intensity of what we say. We can make things feel complex, powerful or exciting just by saying the same sentences quicker. On the opposite, a slow, drawn-out pace gives the audience more time to think and feel what's being said.

To try out your pace, here's a practice sentence, a quote from Dolly Parton: 'If your actions create a legacy that inspires others to dream more, learn more, do more and become more, then, you are an excellent leader.'

Now try this at the slowest pace that still sounds natural. Really give them a chance to ponder your words. Then speed things up, empower your voice to race through the quote. Explore the difference pacing can make and you've got yet another tool in your belt.

Create impact with pauses. Nothing can have an impact quite like saying nothing at all. Impact speakers are masters of well-timed pauses. Pauses allow for reflection on what's been said. Pauses also let you know something important is coming up. Pauses give you a moment to take things in. These can be at the end of a sentence, as a way to fill gaps, or carefully timed between each word to allow things to happen.

Here's a practice sentence from Marcus Aurelius to try your pauses: 'Yes, you can – if you do everything as if it were the last thing you were doing in your life, and stop being aimless, stop letting your emotions override what your mind tells you, stop being hypo-critical, self-centred, irritable.'

When presenting, look for moments to insert pauses that will help create sense and amplify your impact.

Create movement. Imagine a singer performing a powerful song. Visualise it. Is there movement? Even someone like Adele, whose voice gives her licence to just stand there and sing, will emphasise the key moments with her arms and her hands. Performers understand that body language contributes to the flow of a presentation.

It's no different when you're presenting. It's worth pointing out here that this is mostly about in-person presentations, as with online ones, you often need to stay within the narrow field of your webcam.

The best presenters appreciate that when presenting, they are the primary visuals and their slides are a sec-ondary aid. It's easy to lose context of this when the size difference between you and a screen can be five or ten times, but keeping this in mind and harnessing a physical presence when presenting face-to-face will make a big difference.

Live presentations

When it comes to presenting live, here's a three-step process to use the space you have to maximum effect:

1. **Create a grid.** This works best if you've had a chance in rehearsal or preparation to examine the floorplan, but even if not, you can put this into practice. Think of it as a grid. What are the boundaries you are working within? Where will your audience be looking and at what angles will they see you in front of the screen? Ideally, you are looking at three to five key anchor points that you can either mark out with tape or in your head.

2. **Move with purpose.** Draw your audience's eyes and keep energy high. As your presentation starts, you've got your anchors to move to from your starting position. Now it's time to move around with purpose. Do this between groups of content or when it's time to introduce something new. We are looking to create energy, every five to seven minutes at least. If you are using divider slides, these are great prompts to move. Just make sure it's at key points.

3. **Plant your feet and use your arms**. When you move, take a moment and take your time. When you hit your anchor point, use it as a cue to place both feet strongly, face the audience and take a breath. The simple act of planting your feet and

adopting a stable stance will help you project your voice. It will also have the added benefit of helping you cut out some of the nervous, random shuffling and flapping about that can occur.

All of these techniques will build on each other. Paying conscious attention to your body and movement will help keep that feeling of being connected. The next part to think of is how you use your arms as tools to amplify your expressiveness. If your feet are planted, then it's the rest of your body and your arms you need to use.

Be sure to accept that each presenter has their own personality. In order to be authentic, you can't get too caught up in detail here. That's why I recommend starting with whatever tips most stand out to you from this chapter. Implementing all this advice at once gives you way too much to think about.

Just be you. Let the audience know that you are there. The best exercise for this would be to grab your phone, record five minutes of rehearsing, watch and reflect. Look for what you are doing that's helping and powerful and some bad habits that you can strip out.

Just to note

Use the techniques detailed in this chapter the next time you present. As you gain experience and start feeling more comfortable, think about the two or three most important sentences in your presentation. Combine these techniques together to create 'power sentences' – high-impact, pin-drop moments that use your voice to give tremendous meaning to your words.

14
Presentation SOS

There's a good chance this is the first chapter you read if there's a presentation looming and you don't have the time to go through the rest of the book. Maybe you've only got an hour. That's OK. We can work with that. If you need a quick fix, this chapter will tell you what to do. Ideally, with time you can find a way to develop your skills, but for now it's about hacking through.

Be kind to yourself

The first thing you need to do is temper your expectations. Reduce the pressure. Will this be the best presentation you've ever given? Probably not. But with the following steps, it's unlikely to be the worst, either.

You're going to give lots of presentations in the future and this is a great opportunity to practise. Don't set the bar too high and generate anxiety. Just commit to doing good and give yourself more time in the future to create something great. It's going to be OK.

Ten-step checklist

So, what can we learn from impactful presenters that you can immediately use to improve? They follow an order: Structure, Content, Design and Delivery. Knowing that each minute counts, here's a reliable checklist of ten steps to follow now.

1. Think about your audience

Take five to ten minutes to think big. Who are your audience? What are their needs? How will you address them? What is the gift that you are going to share with them? What will be your call to action at the end of the presentation? If you aren't sure and can't answer these questions, reach out with a call or email to someone who knows.

Once you have thought this through, ask yourself the question, 'How will experiencing my presentation change the world for my audience?' This question will narrow down your purpose. Now, in a couple of sentences, write a narrative description of what you're presenting and what the audience will get from it. Get laser sharp and make it interesting. Be specific.

Let's say you're a customer success manager delivering a presentation on your team at an internal leadership conference. The temptation is to take an inwards focus, but think about the audience. Who are they, what do they need to know and how can you serve them?

You might have a bland title like: 'The Customer Success Team'. But take a moment and really think about the perspective that you'd like to take. Do people really want a content dump? What does that imply? Is that interesting? Try to expand on this a bit:

- How Customer Success Supports the Sales Cycle.

- I will share three unique features our team uses for success that anyone can follow.

- A Day in the Life of an Award-Winning Customer Success Team.

- Three things we do differently that any leader can use to improve collaboration and performance.

What this should do is help give clarity on your perspective, generate your title slide and give you the chance to clearly highlight what the 'exchange' between you and the audience will be.

This is part creative and part hard work to get to this stage. It's about packaging the content properly and starting to define a structure. Use this time well; go for a walk and let your mind loose on what this exchange looks like.

2. Pick your length

If you've been set a window to present in and are unsure how long your presentation should be, always aim to go short and finish strong. What we want to counter are two things:

- As we become more comfortable towards the end of the presentation, it's easy to fall into the trap of too much content. It diffuses our message and we lose impact.

- If we run out of time, there's a temptation to rush and thereby fail to create an interactive engagement at the end of our presentation.

As a general approach, look to time your presentation to be 25% shorter than the time allocated and work on an ending to help encourage questions at the end. This will allow time and flexibility for spontaneous discussion if it comes up, and more time for interaction at the end.

3. Give your deck structure with great headlines

I'm assuming here that you've already got a presentation deck of some sort. If you don't, you can craft some simple slides with your title and key points. Keep it stripped back; you will be using these mostly to guide your thoughts and keep you on track.

- **Open PowerPoint and create a great title slide.** Create a simple, clean, bold title slide. Make it impactful, stay away from boring and be unique. Most of all, make sure it helps your audience answer the question in their heads: 'Will this be interesting and give me value? Should I give you my attention?'

- **Create a divider for each section and give them meaningful titles.** Start to group your existing slides into three to five groups. Use sections to divide your content into groups. Scan down your title and divider slides to get a sense of the architecture. Do you have what's needed to answer your title? Does your last slide have a call to action or summary that fits what you've outlined? Create a final slide that gives a key insight or message from each divider slide.

- **Fix your slide headings.** What you want to focus on is the titles or language that you use on each slide. Don't just write plain text. Like newspaper headlines, when you have headings in your slides, try to be interesting. Use active verbs, make promises and build intrigue.

- **Review the flow of your content.** You can now move slides around to fit the content groups you've created. Keep reviewing whether the journey from start to finish is clear. Is each slide in the right place to support the flow and structure of your presentation? Push anything you cut into the appendix or hide the slide.

4. Create a magnificent opening and closing

You already have a tagline or overview of your topic. Think about that first sixty seconds and how you can frame or introduce this. Is there a story, an insight, something that challenges a current perception, some connection most people wouldn't make? Use that and make it interesting. In that first sixty seconds, try to:

- Create a sense of engagement and interest with your audience so that they 'get' you.

- Introduce the exchange of what you will speak about and what they will get from their time with you.

Now think about how your presentation will end. You don't need more content; you need to be closing loops and leaving clear calls to action. Tell people what you want from them. Summarise. Be clear. Be specific.

You want to end gracefully and return the audience back to the moment. If you've done everything well, there will be a natural willingness to engage or even challenge you. That's great. That's the proof point of what you are working towards.

So, start thinking about the last three to five slides in your deck. Think about how you can close off and start to hand the baton back to the audience. Consider what this will look like and leave room to allow it to happen.

5. Fix your design

Start with the mindset that the design is going to be the biggest black hole of your time and one of the biggest risks. Even so, it's important to remember one key truth: *Your deck isn't the presentation, you are.*

You've used the deck to help create the presentation, but it isn't the focus. Your slides are a secondary visual that will help keep you on track to follow a structure and give you prompts to speak to. That said, a bad deck is still going to hamper you, so I'm going to give you a few quick fixes. Your slides may be looking very jumbled with a variety of formatting. Don't waste time perfecting them. We have a series of short examples and some free download resources you can swipe and use.

When it comes to design, all you're going to do are these five things:

- **Transform text to key points.** Whenever you have bullet point content or extended text, condense it down from the whole sentence to a few keywords. Try to condense to prompts and if you have time, with text-heavy slides, animate each different point to fade in on click. For example, 'Half a dozen times a year, we take the team to an offsite to reflect and discuss key client issues and share solutions,' could be, 'Offsites Every Two Months.' That's it. It's a prompt that's easy to understand and helps you then talk to your audience and not read off the screen.

- **Use consistent fonts.** Reduce the jumble of formatting by making sure you have either one font in three sizes or one font for headings and subheadings and another for body copy. Stick to those. With the exception of footers, make sure there are never more than three different sizes on the slides.

- **Trim what you can.** Review all of the content you have on each slide. What doesn't need to be there? What's taking up space and isn't core? White space is your friend. Delete what you can and make sure your alignment helps the key part of each slide stand out.

- **Check your images.** Work through to make sure nothing is too cheesy, stretched or pixilated.

If you have an Office 365 subscription, you can search and find reasonable images within PowerPoint. If not, go to unsplash.com and use wide, thematic search terms to replace the worst images. Make sure you've got divider slides that feel different to the rest of your deck. Save your deck to optimise images and reduce file size.

- **Clear and tidy charts and diagrams.** The goal is to reduce the worst offenders that are actively jarring. These might be charts with rough formatting, screenshots of diagrams or smart art. Make them good enough that people won't laugh at them and you're probably doing better than most!

6. Rehearse and repeat

So far, the aim has been to move as quickly as we can so through to rehearsing. If you are in an SOS situation, the most effective thing you can do as part of your preparation is repetitive rehearsal. You can't achieve a polished, impactful presentation that over-delivers to your audience without working and reworking its delivery. *The challenge here is that the most common way we rehearse is the least effective.*

When it comes time to rehearse, move away from your desk, place your computer away in the corner of the room and start practising delivery by not staring at your screen – only glancing at it. Invest in a remote clicker if you can, even if you are presenting online.

Move, think on your feet and practise your tone, pace and reflection points. Start to feel the flow. Stop and fix the details on your slides.

Then do it again. As much as you can. The more you rehearse, the less nervous and more polished you will be and the more your audience will be willing to invest. Very quickly, as you rehearse, you will feel your delivery improving and your confidence rising.

However, that's only level one. To reach a higher level of impact, set up your phone, record your rehearsal and review it. Make some adjustments and then do it again. Viewing footage is a fantastic insight into understanding your physiology when presenting. It will reveal how you move, your gestures and your interactions with your slides and how you use your voice.

When you commit to rehearsing your presentation, no matter how uncomfortable it is, you will increase your impact.

7. Plan interaction

Interaction is the key to having an impact. High-impact presenters are finely tuned in the art of doing this by asking great questions – not the slide with a clipart question mark, but well thought out, purposeful questions that serve a specific purpose.

Questions are a tool you always have available however you're presenting. They also serve the purpose of changing the energy of an audience. Instead of just sitting there watching you, they're going to be active and engage with you. We are naturally wired to fill silences, so by asking a question and waiting patiently, there is a natural urge to actually think and give it a try.

The secret to using questions and creating interaction is to first have the audience on your side when you are fresh into a presentation and in the zone. But just like you're trying to manage your nerves, it takes confidence for someone to speak up, so you'll only get engagement when people trust you and feel safe.

Rather than listing out a set of questions, a more effective way is to start with a purpose as a prompt and then you can craft the question to fit your own need based on your own content. Here are two different types of question that you can quickly use.

Staging questions. Set the stage to introduce a new answer or solution. Create context or a sense of importance around your topic, for example, 'What was the best x?' or, 'What if we could do y?'

Instead of telling people, 'We need to do this,' ask them, 'What do we need to do?' and guide them to the right answers.

Rolling questions. The rolling question technique involves taking an audience member's question and redirecting it to another person or group of people to encourage discussion. It might look a bit like this:

> Presenter: 'Who can think of any problems with x?'
> Audience member: 'Well, one problem might be y.'
> Presenter: 'Absolutely! So does anyone know how we could get around that?'

Using questions is a powerful technique for inter-action. However, you are also giving up some con-trol over the presentation. Be prepared to step in if needed, to move things back to your presentation if things start to flow away. An effective way to do that:

- Acknowledge the person.

- Restate what they've said.

- Offer to have a detailed discussion after the presentation.

- Get back on track by stating where you left off and what's next.

Finally, make sure you plan where you will ask questions and how you will respond to the common answers you might expect to hear.

8. Master the setup

Set up a Zoom or Teams meeting with just you to check your background, lighting, audio and perspective of the camera are on point. Remove the background distractions, place a lamp in front of you and if your internal microphone isn't great, use quality headphones or AirPods to ensure you have consistent, clean audio.

Now I'm going to share one tip to make things feel a bit more natural. I am well aware that it's going to sound strange, even stupid, but it genuinely works. Cut out a series of faces and paste them to the top of your monitor, near to your camera. *I know, I know*, but just try it. You'll be amazed how it reduces awkwardness by introducing some real life to the situation.

- **Find a natural body position.** This is usually standing up instead of sitting down. Standing up creates a similar feeling to presenting live by allowing expressive body language and gestures.

- **Adjust slides for online presenting.** Online delivery means less detail on slides and a higher frequency of them. Try to make sure you are regularly moving through your slides.

9. Control your physiology

You need to be sharp and effective, not overwhelmed. It's time to take control of your physiology. Have a glass of water. Even the most experienced presenters will feel the nerves that you are feeling right now, so embrace them. All they mean is that you're about to do something important and you care about the result. That's a good thing.

This is a technique used by many world leaders and it only takes twelve seconds.

Any time you feel nerves taking over and your heart rate starting to creep up, give yourself a moment to look in the mirror, take a deep breath, move and smile:

- Breathe, move, smile

- Breathe

- Move

- Smile

It takes twelve seconds to do this three times. Feel the amazing difference it can make. What's happening is that you are starting to control your body's biochemistry. Your smile is reducing cortisol – the stress chemical that drives up your heart rate. Your breathwork is activating your parasympathetic nervous system, taking down your nerves and making you feel calm. It's so easy. Just twelve seconds will make a difference, but you can try this technique five or ten times leading up to your presentation. It might sound silly, but this simple practice can boost your confidence and set the stage for a powerful presentation.

10. After it's over

OK, so this step is more about distribution than delivery.

There's an ongoing conflict between optimising a presentation for live delivery compared to sending someone a PDF of your presentation. Sending someone a deck by itself isn't a presentation, it's a document. There is no personal element, it's hard to engage with and is likely to be skim read.

The best hybrid solution is to use Loom and send your deck. If you haven't used it yet, Loom is a super-helpful productivity tool that lets you screen record along with your camera. It is very simple to set up and use.

So, if you are going to send someone a copy of your presentation, record a Loom introduction with your slides on screen as you talk. You've got a few different ways to set it up, so you can then choose whatever arrangement you like. Plan what you'd like to say. Then hit record.

When complete, you can edit it in Loom and send it to the client along with the deck. Clients can watch at different speeds, it has a transcript, and you also get an email once they view it.

Just to note

Polish and repeat.

Wrap Up

You made it! This is far from the end of your presenting journey, but you've completed a significant step. With what you've learned over the course of this book, you have the tools at your disposal to start improving your skills as a presenter.

Countless presentations take place every day. You can picture exactly what the vast majority of them are like: stumbling presenters, dated graphics, a slow drift into boredom for an unenthusiastic audience.

No excitement, no engagement, and, ultimately, no impact. Most of these presentations won't make a difference – the world before and after them is entirely unchanged. Just by reading this, you've made a commitment to change that. And now you know how.

It begins with mindset

That's what sets apart the high-impact presenters from the rest. They take the time to think about the audience and consider the all-important exchange.

They don't just ask for your attention without promising anything in return. Presentations should serve their audience. Start with that and you're on the right track. Move away from slide thinking and take your audience on a journey.

You are going to be judged, whether you put the effort into your presentation or not. So why wouldn't you take the time to give your audience something and build a positive impression of yourself in return? Even better, why not have a specific goal for your presentation, a defined call to action, and build towards that moment?

The 5 Power Principles to remember

I say 'remember', but I mean 'keep in mind'. I'm not going to test you on them. There's no exam! Use this book, refer to it next time you're building a presentation.

The principles will gradually become second nature, but you won't get them all perfect from the beginning. That's fine. Chances are your next presentation isn't a TED Talk. Incremental improvement is absolutely the goal. Getting a little better each time might not ever turn you into a professional presenter, but it will still make you better than almost everyone else. Here are those Power Principles:

1. The audience is number one.

2. Start with the end in mind.

3. Be authentically you.

4. Assume apathy.

5. Prepare to overdeliver.

OK, just a little test: can you read those principles and recall what they mean? If not, maybe flip or scroll back through the book and refresh your memory.

The 4D Process

With the right mindset in place, you will understand how you should be approaching your role as a presenter. That's all well and good, but you still have to actually sit down and make the PowerPoint too. That's where our proven process comes into play.

The 4D Process has, unsurprisingly, four steps that all start with D:

1. **Define** the structure.

2. **Develop** dynamic content.

3. **Design** distinctive visuals.

4. **Deliver** with confidence.

By working through them in this order, you'll work out the flow of the story you're telling, focus on the essential content for it, bolster your message with eye-catching design and manage your nerves to step up and achieve.

It starts with your next presentation

Taking all this advice on board isn't going to instantly make your next presentation a world-class, life-changing masterpiece (although if it does, I want some credit), but you've got a chance of delivering something better than average – something that might just have an impact. It'll also give you valuable feedback on where you've improved and what you still have to work on.

That's the real key. Deliver, analyse, improve, repeat.

Step by step, slide by slide, you'll start to make an impact. On yourself. On your audience. On the world.

Good luck!

References

Adegbuyi, F., 'How to Learn Anything with the Feynman Technique' (no date). Retrieved from https://todoist.com/inspiration/feynman-technique on April 9, 2023.

Aurelius, M. (2006). *Meditations* (translated by M. Hammond). Penguin Classics.

Bariso, J., 'Jeff Bezos Says This Is Why He Banned PowerPoint at Amazon. It's a Lesson in How to Think' (December 21, 2023). Retrieved from www.inc-aus.com/justin-bariso/amazon-jeff-bezos-powerpoint-meetings-how-to-think.html on March 11, 2023.

Bumiller, E., 'We Have Met the Enemy and He Is PowerPoint' (April 27, 2010). Retrieved from www.nytimes.com/2010/04/27/world/27powerpoint.html on March 11, 2023.

Champion, N., TEDx Talk, '10 Seconds of Courage: Life Lessons from a Fighter' (May 6, 2015). Retrieved from www.youtube.com/watch?v=r1Zfscuv_YE&t=3s on August 1, 2023.

Hanson, J., 'The 30-point rule, and other tips to prepare a killer presentation that will keep your audience off their phones' (August 31, 2022). Retrieved from www.forbes.com/sites/janehanson/2022/08/31/the-30-point-rule-and-other-tips-to-prepare-a-killer-presentation-that-will-keep-your-audience-off-their-phones on March 8, 2024.

Horvath, Dr. J. C. (2019). *Stop Talking, Start Influencing: 12 Insights from Brain Science to Make Your Message Stick.* Exisle Publishing.

Parton, D. (1997), cited in *The Most Important Thing I Know.* Andrews McMeel Publishing.

Rogan, J., 'The Joe Rogan Experience: #1247 – Andy Stumpf' (February, 2019). Retrieved from: https://open.spotify.com/episode/1LDQIC3goOJZ2jKxCHvvbc on March 8, 2024.

Sinek, S., TEDx Talk, 'Start with why – how great leaders inspire action' (September 29, 2009). Retrieved from www.youtube.com/watch?v=u4ZoJKF_VuA on January 17, 2024.

Yousafzai, M., 'Malala Yousafzai: 16th birthday speech at the United Nations' (July 12, 2013). Retrieved from https://malala.org/newsroom/malala-un-speech on January 21, 2024.

Acknowledgements

Writing this book has been a rewarding challenge, and it is with immense gratitude that I express my appreciation to those who have made it possible.

First and foremost, my family have always given me their unwavering support both for writing this book and for PDCo. I'm well aware that deadlines don't always align with family time! All I can say is thank you so much Sandra, Henry, Sam and Niamh.

Rakhi and Julia, we've been on this journey together for a long time and we've created a special partnership along the way. Your hard work, dedication, patience and creative thinking through many, many projects over the years have helped shape the approach we've been able to develop. Thanks also to Sufi, Angela, Nicko, Eric, Yuki and Denzel for supporting them!

To the PDCo Team: Agung, Cynthia, Ozzy and Rio. You've worked incredibly hard against countless tight deadlines so that we could help our clients to have an impact. It's a joy to work with a dedicated and talented team, I'm incredibly grateful.

Then, to all those wonderful clients who have trusted us with their presentations and believed in our process. Special thanks to Kellie, Daryl, Peter and Kerrie.

Thank you to my remarkable editor Jake – you were able to take something very rough and perform your magic to turn it into something far better.

Thank you for the support crew that are always a call away Nigel, Dan, Liam, Jody, Lester and Des. Pete – for the amazing work on developing how PDCo looks to the world, we will always be grateful for your expertise.

Finally, a message for everyone else reading this. To the readers who embark on this journey of self-improvement with the aim of creating better presentations, I extend my sincere wishes for your success. I hope that the insights shared in these pages empower you to communicate better than ever with your clients, team and the world.

In closing, this book is a testament to the collective effort of those who believe in the power of effective communication. May it inspire presenters to embrace their potential.

With gratitude

Kris

The Author

Kris started his career in the banking sector before becoming the founder and director of Presentation Design Co and a certified Platinum Prezi Expert. Along with his team, he has worked to construct and design thousands of presentations for clients such as Toyota, Coca Cola, Qantas and the Australian Government since 2012. Based on his experience working first-hand with hundreds of presenters, Kris noticed similarities in what resonated across different professions, industries and locations – and it's not what we think!

This sparked his discovery that despite presentations' critical importance, there was very little scientific evidence for the approach presenters took. Instead, they relied on a 'do what I say', guru-type approach – or often, guessing what they should be doing.

Today, Kris and his team are the go-to presentation design and development team for Australia's most sought-after speakers, high-ranking executives and start-up entrepreneurs.

You can follow Kris and his team:

🌐 www.presentationdesign.co

📘 www.facebook.com/pdcoaus

💼 www.linkedin.com/in/kris-flegg

▶️ www.youtube.com/@pdcoaus